the
MICHIGAN
book of
BESTS

an eclectic barrage of great places to go and things to know

by
Gary W. Barfknecht

Friede Publications

THE MICHIGAN BOOK OF BESTS

Copyright, 1999, by Gary W. Barfknecht

This book may not be reproduced in whole or part
by mimeograph or any other means without permission.

Friede Publications
P.O. Box 217
Davison, Michigan 48423

Printed in the United States of America

First Printing, September, 1999

ISBN 0-923756-20-5

For Elva

my newspaper bag lady

Of course you wont find the "Best Couple in Gaylord" in this book. The author felt it was too close to call between us & you while you still were here. Now that you are on your way to T.C. The field is open for us to be in later editions. Maybe after a few years of retirement you can write your own book or a rebuttal to this!!

All photos are by the author except where otherwise indicated

May the sun be on your shoulders & the wind at your backs. Love,

Butch & Joan

OTHER BOOKS BY GARY W. BARFKNECHT

Unexplained Michigan Mysteries
Ultimate Michigan Adventures
Mich-Again's Day
Michillaneous (out of print)
Michillaneous II (out of print)
Murder, Michigan (out of print)

FOREWORD

This book was massaged out of a brain cramp I suffered during a step back in time followed by a jump to a conclusion. The spasm struck in May 1996 as I reflected upon my author/publisher career while perusing the nearly 3,000 titles listed in a catalog put out by my firm's main distributor, who specializes in Michigan and Great Lakes area books.

I created Friede Publications in 1981 out of necessity when — I'm embarrassed to say that I'm no longer embarrassed to say — not for the first time I had done things bass ackwards. I had spent two years researching and writing a trivia book titled *Michillaneous* only to discover there were no potential publishers for it. There were a few excellent Michigan-based university and religious presses, but none interested in doing a fun, light, overall look at our incredibly interesting and diverse state. So I successfully self-published and went on to bring five more of my books into print plus 17 by eight other Michigan authors and illustrators.

Preparing a book for print back then was tedious, time-consuming and unforgiving. Galley sheets arrived from typesetting bureaus as toilet-paper-like rolls that had to be unscrolled, flattened, scissor- and exacto-blade cut and sliced, coated on the back with hot wax, and "pasted" onto grid-marked layout "boards." Typesetting errors required resetting lines, then cutting and pasting them over the originals. Layout changes and corrections meant peeling off part or all of a page and starting over. The labor-intensive process was grueling or, if you didn't do it yourself, prohibitively expensive, which I'm convinced is why for many years few others joined me in the Michigan small-press pool.

But with the advent of affordable, sophisticated-yet-easy-to-use computer desktop publishing hardware and software in the 1990s, practically anyone who could move and click a mouse was a potential publisher. The result was an explosion of self-published and small-press books.

The shrapnel in Michigan, I observed from the catalog, had scattered wide and penetrated deep. Art, architecture, history, humor, outdoor recreation, nature, spectator sports, travel, and cooking were among just the catalog's general contents categories. The shipwreck section alone offered nearly 40 different books. And interspersed throughout the 100-plus pages were Michigan-specific books devoted exclusively to salamanders, lichens, highway bridges, log marks, quilts, snakes, and other formerly esoteric subjects.

Not only had every Michigan target been hit, it seemed, but occasionally overkilled. There simply were no Michigan subjects, no fresh angles, no new perspectives left, I concluded, for me to either write about or publish.

Trying to rid the painful thought by rubbing my temples caused — I later learned from the New-Age Neurological Institute — a surge of electrical activity in my brain that instead of triggering yet another brownout, initiated a minor epiphany. I suddenly recognized that many of the Michigan and other regional books in the catalog — despite their wide-range, diversity and disparity — shared an extraordinarily simple, narrow focus. Implicit though rarely expressed in their titles was the word *best*. Our Friede Publications *Fish Michigan* series, for example, doesn't specifically say so, but out of the state's 11,000 inland lakes, the author details the 300 he rates *best* for angling. *The Divers Guide to Michigan* doesn't feature *every* place to go under the state's vast Great and inland lakes waters, only the best. And even the encyclopedic *Buildings of Michigan* focuses only on the best Michigan examples of various architectural styles.

And sharpening *my* newly discovered focus, I also quickly recognized that even the plethora of books in my distributor's catalog barely skimmed Michigan's crème de la crème. What I could do — what I now *had* to do — was find Michigan's best fill-in-the-blanks-until-exhaustive-or-exhausted, strip them down to their most alluring essence, and reveal them in a new, possibly mesmerizing light.

I did post three areas "off limits": I would not include people (except for what turned out to be a half dozen or so too-good-to-leave-out exceptions). I knew that, even by itself, a collection of brief bios of Michigan's most colorful characters past and present could be as thick as an unabridged dictionary and possibly as exciting. Ditto for sports. Nor would I play God with "life essentials." I'm not qualified to determine and recommend, for examples, places to get the best health care, housing, legal and financial advice, or education. And not knowing the credibility of or criteria, methodology, and agendas behind ubiquitous "top-10 or -100" lists by magazines, newspapers, organizations, and other "experts," I'm too cynical and skeptical to pass them along as gospel.

Next, I had to objectify the almost-always-subjective nature of what determines a "best." I decided that anything that stood out out or stood alone for any positive reason — biggest, most-popular,

rarest, most unique, easiest, most-spectacular, for examples — was a good candidate.

Eyes, ears, mouth and mind wide open, I then spent three years searching, researching, and re-researching. I rummaged through boxes and file cabinets full of Michigan materials I had accumulated over 20 years. I checked out — figuratively and almost literally — every contemporary Michigan book at the State of Michigan Library. Daily, my fingers turned black while turning the pages of a half dozen different newspapers. I surfed the web, scoured CD ROM indexes, reviewed a sweepstakes clearing house-worth of magazines, logged hundreds of 10-10-UPAY calls, and traveled between Hell and Paradise.

Finally it was my pleasure to turn what I found into what I hope you will agree is a fun, fascinating and, yes, even useful read.

Please enjoy Michigan at its best.

Gary W. Barfknecht
Petoskey, Michigan

CONTENTS

DIVERSIONS

MOST-EXCITING ELEVATOR RIDE

MARRIOTT HOTEL. Renaissance Center, Detroit.

The breathtaking trip to the top of Michigan's tallest building is a floor-a-second shot 700-plus feet up the *outside* of the gleaming Renaissance Center tower in a small, nearly all-glass, see-through tube.

(313) 568-8000

EASIEST SHOOT DOWN A CHUTE

MUSKEGON STATE PARK. Muskegon.

During scheduled winter hours here, you can — without appointment or experience — rent a helmet, get instruction then, while lying flat on your back, pilot a tiny one-person sled down an ice-covered, wood-walled luge.

(231) 744-9629 (in season only)

COOLEST TOBOGGAN RUN

Oakland County Parks

THE FRIDGE. Waterford Oaks County Park, Waterford.

During an initial 55-foot plunge down the twin tracks of the state's only refrigerated toboggan run, four-passenger, Amish-made, red-oak sleds build up speeds to 30 mph then hurtle riders on a 30-second thrill run through 1,000 feet of dips, dives and straightaways. Refrigeration units built into the flumes of the $1.7-million structure assure icy-smooth sledding from Thanksgiving to March.

(248) 858-0906

MOST-POPULAR SLED-DOG RACE

U.P. 200 SLED DOG CHAMPIONSHIP.

As many as 30,000 spectators crowd into downtown Marquette the second weekend of February each winter to cheer the start and finish of one of the country's finest mid-distance sled-dog races. And thousands more fans greet mushers and their animals at checkpoints and layover spots along the grueling 240-mile Marquette-Chatham-Rapid River-Escanaba-Gwinn-Marquette course.

(800) 544-4321   www.marquettecountry.org

BEST PLACE TO WATCH FULL-CONTACT JOUSTING

MICHIGAN RENAISSANCE FESTIVAL.
Holly.
Knights wearing authentic suits of metal armor, astride horses and armed with wood stage lances put on realistic jousting performances three times daily during this well-known late-summer/fall festival's seven-weekend-long celebration of 16th century life.

(800) 601-4848   www.renaissancefest.com

Michigan Renaissance Festival

MOST-EXCITING AIR SHOW

SELFRIDGE AIR NATIONAL GUARD BASE.
Harrison Township.

Nearly 100 aircraft and their crews perform during the state's best combination of precision and stunt flying plus static ground displays. Pre-WWII planes, state-of-the-art Stealth fighters, a tiny "Tweety Bird" trainer, a behemoth C5 Galaxy (the largest plane in the Air Force), seemingly out-of-control stunt pilots, and the disciplined, heart-stopping Air Force Thunderbirds are among recent performers at the annual summer weekend-long event.

(810) 307-6999

MOST CREDIBLE, INCREDIBLE UFO SIGHTINGS

One of the most-remarkable and widely publicized UFO events — anywhere, ever — occurred in southeast Michigan in March 1966. In a week-long series of incidents, dozens of law enforcement officers, Selfridge Air Force Base personnel, and several hundred reliable citizens witnessed elliptical, brightly lit UFOs dip, hover, fly in formation and land.

Those who got close looks said the objects were football shaped and car size, with quilted or pitted surfaces and flashing red and green lights. A civilian consultant was sent by the Air Force to investigate but was practically laughed out of the area when he attributed the phenomena to "swamp gas." To this day there have been no other explanations or sightings.

BEST PLACE TO WATCH KITE PILOTS GET LIT

GREAT LAKES SPORT KITE CHAMPIONSHIP.
Grand Haven.

More than 100 of North America's top stunt kite pilots compete and perform on the beaches at Grand Haven State park on a mid-May weekend each year. What is billed as one of the world's largest kite events, includes a spectacular "night fly," when participants stage a mass launch of kites and lines lit with tiny colored bulbs.

(616) 846-7501   www.mackinawkiteco.com

BEST PLACE TO TELL YOUR CHILD TO GO FLY A KITE

KITEFEST. Kalamazoo.

Michigan's largest family kite festival, held annually the last weekend of April, includes two days of free kite-making workshops for children, plus a workshop, demonstration and competition for sport kites.

(616) 383-8778

MOST-SPECTACULAR BALLOON LAUNCH

TEAM U.S. NATIONALS
HOT-AIR BALLOON CHAMPIONSHIP. Battle Creek.

On opening night of the state's biggest ballooning event, a mass launch of several hundred technicolored hot-air craft jams Battle Creek's sky lanes like freeway traffic on a holiday weekend. The hours- and miles-long air parade includes several distinctively designed promotional balloons, such as a Burger King Whopper and an incredible 145-foot-tall Disney creation, "Castle in the Clouds."

(616) 962-0592
www.bcballoons.com

U.S. Nationals Hot-Air Balloon Championship

BEST STATE PARK TO WATCH BALLOON LAUNCHES

ISLAND LAKE RECREATION AREA. Brighton.

The Meadow Picnic Area here is the only balloonport in a Michigan state park.

(248) 229-7067

BEST STATE PARK TO PLAY TENNIS

BEWABIC. Crystal Falls.

Incongruously set in this isolated, hilly, densely forested Upper Peninsula park are the only two tennis courts in the state-run system.

(906) 875-3324

MOST-INTENSE PUBLIC/PRIVATE PLAYLAND PATCHWORK

A roughly 7-square-mile area west of Mears takes in Silver Lake State Park plus privately owned commercial enterprises that combine to form "a huge playground," says Tom Powers in *Michigan State and National Parks* (Friede Publications). Spread over fragmented and scattered state park plots are enormous sand dunes, an historic lighthouse on a scenic stretch of Lake Michigan beach, a campground, an ORV area (p. 31), and a beautiful inland lake offering swimming, fishing and boating.

Intermixed, abutting and surrounding are private-sector water slides, bumper boats and cars, video and game arcades, food concessions and restaurants, golf, a trout farm, Jellystone Park, a dune-buggy ride (p. 31), riding stables, and sailboat, sailboard, jet ski, pedalboat, bicycle, ORV and canoe rentals.

BEST AMUSEMENT PARK

MICHIGAN'S ADVENTURE. Muskegon.

The main draws to Michigan's largest fun park complex are six roller coasters (including the nation's third-largest wooden coaster) and a water-theme area that features 24 slides (including the state's longest), three wave pools (including the state's largest), an enclosed raft ride called The Mineshaft, a tubing "river," and a swimming beach. The Frog Hopper, Falling Star, Hi-Striker, Half-Pint Paradise, a go-kart track, and an 18-hole miniature golf course are other of the more than 40 thrilling to gentle rides and attractions spread over 200-acres.

(231) 766-3377   www.miadventure.com

MERRIEST GO-ROUNDS

There are eight vintage (circa 1900-1925) carousels around in the state in varying states of storage, restoration and operation. The three biggest and best fully restored working rides are located at:

VAN ANDEL MUSEUM CENTER. Grand Rapids.

Surrounded by a glass-walled pavilion overlooking the Grand River, this 3-row, 55-foot-in-diameter 1928 Spillman Carousel — featuring 44 horses, six menagerie animals, two chariots, 1,200 incandescent lights, and its original 1908 Wurlitzer organ — carries riders year-round.

(616) 456-3977   www.grmuseum.org

GREENFIELD VILLAGE. Dearborn.

More than 300,000 people a year ride an artfully restored 1913 Barbary Coast 3-row carousel complete with 21 jumping and eight standing horses, three chariots, one tub, and an 11-animal menagerie that includes zebras, giraffes, dogs and a sea monster. Music blasts from a 1900 Wurlitzer band organ.

(800) 835-5237   www.hfmgv.org

HISTORIC CROSSROADS VILLAGE. Flint.

In a far corner of this 19th-century museum village is a working 3-row carousel created in 1912 by Charles Parker, "America's Amusement King." The ride, complete with an Artizan self-playing band organ, features 40 horses, including four metal kiddie-size jumping ponies with a nanny's bench behind them.

(810) 736-7100   www.geneseecountyparks.org

LARGEST VIRTUAL-GAMES ARCADE

GAMEWORKS. Auburn Hills.

At this huge, high-tech, smart-card-(not coin-)operated indoor playland you can climb onto or into real-time simulations of snowboards, Indy car shells, motorcycle bodies, stock car seats, skateboards, downhill and water skiis, hydroplane hulls, wave runners, mountain bikes that realistically slide, bump, jostle, skim and soar as you maneuver them through computer-generated courses projected onto large screens.

More than 225 attractions at this two-level, 35,000 square-foot adjunct to Great Lakes Crossing (p. 14) also include networked multiplayer games,

pool tables, pinball machines, lots of Atari, Sega and other standard-issue video games plus two bars and a restaurant.

(248) 745-9675

CHOICEST MUSEUM ARCADE

MARVIN'S MARVELOUS MECHANICAL MUSEUM AND EMPORIUM. Farmington Hills.

Nearly a century's worth of beautifully restored, working coin-operated games, rides, and other mechanical amusements are interspersed with antique posters, neon signs, sideshow banners and trendy, state-of-the-art video and virtual games in this colorful, noisy combination arcade/indoor amusement park/museum. Patrons from toddlers through seniors choose from more than 300 fascinating vintage, penny-arcade devices such as kiddie rides, fortune tellers, love meters, grip testers, pinball machines, table hockey, peep-card shows, pellet-plinking pistols, and lots of mechanical metal-jawed "prize-grabbers" plus an array of digital coin-grabbers.

(248) 626-5020

MOST-MOVING MOVING-PICTURES

DETROIT SCIENCE CENTER OMNIMAX THEATER. Detroit.

At the state's only IMAX theatre, you *feel* like you're in the middle of the action when a 70mm projector fills a 67-foot-in-diameter, domed screen with wraparound motion, sound and color. Rolling and diving in a supersonic jet; moving over, under, between and through Antarctic ice; or standing at the edge of an erupting volcano are among the ever-changing thrills movie-goers experience.

(313) 577-8400

MOST AUTO-MATED MOVIES

FORD WYOMING DRIVE-IN. Dearborn.

With eight separate screens simultaneously showing movies from dusk to dawn, this is the largest drive-in complex in Michigan, according to Jim DuFresne in *Michigan Off the Beaten Path* (The Globe Pequot Press). "On a good weekend," adds the author, "there will be more than 2,000 cars and somewhere between 5,000-8,000 watching (the films)."

(313) 846-6910

MOST-VIEWED FILM VENUE

STAR SOUTHFIELD ENTERTAINMENT CENTER. Southfield.

Annually more than 3 million movie-goers buy tickets at this 20-screen, 6,000-seat complex, placing it at or near the top of the list of the country's and sometimes the *world's* most-attended theaters.

(248) 372-2222   www.star-theatres.com

MOST-PLENTIFUL PROJECTIONS

STAR GREAT LAKES CROSSING. Auburn Hills.

Michigan biggest movie megaplex boasts 25 screens; 5,200 stadium-style, high-back, rocking-chair seats; floor-to-ceiling screens; state-of-the-art digital sound systems; and a minimall's worth of food-court and movie-merchandise choices. The $30 million complex opened in 1999 as part of the state's newest and biggest combination shopping/entertainment mall (p. 14).

(248) 454-0366

MOST-SPECTACULAR CASINOS

Two of Michigan's 17 Indian-run casinos have developed into standout, stand-alone, state-of-the-art gaming/entertainment/convention/shopping/dining/lodging complexes.

At the two, gamblers have the 24-hour-a-day, seven-days-a-week opportunity to pull the handles of several thousand slot machines, ask for hits at hundreds of blackjack tables, and try their luck at video and real poker, keno, bingo, and roulette plus a credit-card-limit's worth of exotic games.

Away from the gaming action but also on site, guests can retire to large, new hotels with rooms ranging from economy to luxury; eat in a choice of restaurants with menus ranging from buffet to fine dining; browse through upscale shops; absorb Native American culture in art galleries; and in Vegas-like lounges and theatres, take in performances by name entertainers such as BB King, Aretha Franklin, Don Rickles, Travis Tritt, Wayne Newton, Loretta Lynn and Roy Clark.

SOARING EAGLE CASINO. Mt. Pleasant.

This mega-resort — the second-largest Indian-run casino in the nation, the Midwest's largest casino complex, and the state's only AAA four-diamond-rated gambling center — attracts an average of 15,000 visitors a day during the week and 40,000 on weekends.

(888) 732-4537   www.sagchip.org

VEGAS KEWADIN. Sault Ste. Marie.

For its sprawling size, this flagship of five Chippewa-run Upper Peninsula casinos has a reputation for being relaxed, laid back and friendly.

(800) 539-2346   www.kewadin.com

HOTTEST CASINO BEACH

CHIP-IN ISLAND RESORT & CASINO. Harris.

Children of guests staying at a 113-room motel in this tropical-themed complex can play year-round in a small, indoor, pool-side, heated sand beach.

(800) 682-6040   www.chipincasino.com

MOST-VENERABLE VINTAGE SPORTS BAR

LINDELL AC. Detroit.

At this mother of *all* sports bars — Michigan's, maybe the country's first — you can absorb the memories and memorabilia of Detroit's pro sports legends in their favorite place to celebrate wins, mourn losses, relax and even fight. Established in 1949, the unpretentious tavern is a classic gallery of uniforms, scrapbooks, autographed photos, sticks, bats, balls, gloves and other equipment (including a bronzed jockstrap) donated by such famous regulars as Billy Martin, Gordie Howe, Al Kaline, Dave Bing and Alex Karras.

(313) 964-1122

MOST-REWARDING PLACE TO DOWN DOGS

CORNER BAR. Rockford.

Eat a dozen chili dogs in four hours here, and your name will be engraved on a tiny brass plate and added to several thousand others in the Hot Dog Hall of Fame. Or go for the world record — 42½ dogs in four hours.

(616) 866-9866

BEST BAR TO WATCH THE WINGS

THE FIVE HOLE. Detroit.

Cameras and microphones strategically placed around Joe Louis Arena relay Detroit Red Wing home games to this third-floor hockey-theme bar next door to the Fox Theatre. A giant projection TV screen brings the action almost as close-up as rink-side, while stacks of surround-sound speakers blast the roar of fans, thuds from crunching body checks, R-rated remarks by players on receiving end of same, and other actual game sounds.

(313) 965-2222

WILDEST DRINKING DECOR

THE ANTLERS. Sault Ste. Marie.

More than 300 mounted animals — including a 15-foot boa constrictor wrapped around a support pillar, a pride of lions, and a two-headed calf — plus scores of antlers, a full-size birch-bark canoe, and collectibles cover just about every square foot of wall and ceiling space at this small, popular 75-year old bar/restaurant.

(906) 632-3571

MOST-POPULAR WAY-OFF-THE-BEATEN-PATH TAVERN

ELBOW LAKE BAR. Meredith.

Thousands of hunters, snowmobilers, skiers, berry pickers, and the regions cottage-owners leave main roads miles behind to eat classic bar food and relax in this intimate, family oriented log tavern on the shore of its namesake lake. Furnishings are mismatches. Entertainment consists of a two-for-a-quarter country-music jukebox, one pool table, one pinball machine, and a 1953 dime-per-play wood table-shuffleboard. And walls and ceilings are decorated with license plates, 500 hats, plastic and real mounted deer heads and fish, and other Americana.

Yet, or as a result, since its 1949 opening the former hunting cabin's reputation has spread, mostly by word of mouth, to the point where governors' and other elected and appointed officials' limos and tour buses pull up unexpectedly; corporations reserve the small, one-room facility as a head-clearing place to hold meetings; and recently, newspapers, television stations, and magazines have all featured the self-described "Mayberry-like" throwback.

(517) 539-9582

MOST-VENERABLE JAZZ CLUB

BAKER'S KEYBOARD LOUNGE. Detroit.

Since 1934, what may be the world's oldest live-jazz club has been the Michigan venue of choice for a long list of local and national jazz greats including Sarah Vaughan, John Coltrane, Cab Calloway, Cannonball Adderley, Sonny Stitt, Dexter Gordon, Pat Flowers, Miles Davis, Oscar Peterson, Mel Torme and Dave Brubeck.

(313) 345-6300

FOLKSIEST CLUB

THE ARK. Ann Arbor.

This second-story off-campus institution is one of the country's premier places to sing, play, hear and learn about the world's folk music. More than 250 quality concerts each year feature a wide range of regional and international performers, including many well-known artists who like to break in their tour acts in the intimate, friendly environment.

(734) 761-1451   www.a2ark.org

THE NIGHTCLUB THAT LAUGHS LONGEST, LAUGHS BEST

MARK RIDLEY'S COMEDY CASTLE. Royal Oak.

For more than 20 years, audiences at Michigan's leading and original showcase of comedy have laughed at more than 3,500 upcoming and established comics, including Rosie O'Donnell, Jerry Seinfeld, Paul Reiser, Dennis Miller, Tim Allen and Dave Coulier.

(248) 542-9900

MOST-MAGICAL GATHERING

ABBOTT'S MAGIC GET-TOGETHER. Colon.

Each August thousands of professional and amateur magicians from all over the world flock to Michigan's magic capital, where they conduct formal lectures and demonstrations, hold magic contests, entertain at four evening shows, plus perform an unknown number of impromptu sleight-of-hands on street corners.

(616) 432-3235   www.net-link.net/abbottmagic

GREATEST HOLIDAY BRIGHTENERS

WAYNE COUNTY LIGHTFEST. Westland to Dearborn.

More than a million sparkling lights arranged into nearly 40 giant displays — including a supersize Santa sleigh and parachuting and prancing reindeer — illuminate 4½ winding miles of Hines Drive every December. The giant glow is billed as the Midwest's largest holiday light show.

(734) 261-1990

INTERNATIONAL FESTIVAL OF LIGHTS. Battle Creek.

Each December, downtown Cereal City is transformed into a brilliant walk-through after-dark spectacle, with more than a million colored lights adorning buildings and forming 400 specially created holiday displays.

(800) 397-2240   www.battlecreekvisitors.org

PREMIER PYROTECHNICS

HUDSON'S FIREWORKS. Detroit.

North America's largest one-night fireworks display — 20,000 pounds of colorful, controlled explosives packed into 10,000 devices that explode high above the Detroit River nonstop for 30 minutes — draws more than a million spectators to the opening night of the annual International Freedom Festival.

(800) 338-7648   www.visitdetroit.com

FIREWORKS FESTIVAL. BAY CITY.

The state's longest-lasting Fourth of July blast takes place over three nights when, in a pair of 20-minute shows and one 40-minute boomfest finale, a total of more than 20,000 colorful shells whistle, thud, thunder, spiral, and starburst over the heads of more than 600,000 spectators.

(888) 229-8696   (517) 892-2264

GREATEST PARADE

THANKSGIVING DAY PARADE. Detroit.

At 9 a.m. each Thanksgiving Day, as many as a million spectators line Woodward Avenue to watch a 2.5-mile-long procession of 40 floats, 150 clowns, 25 marching bands, a half dozen equestrian units, giant helium-filled balloon characters and caricatures, and drill teams, unicyclists, acrobats, and other "specialty" units. The holiday institution, held since 1948 and nationally televised most years, has often been called "America's Thanksgiving Day Parade."

(313) 923-7400.

MOST-POPULAR TRAFFIC TIE-UP

WOODWARD DREAM CRUISE. Detroit to Pontiac.

The world's largest single-day car cruise is a 12-hour bumper-to-bumper parade of fascinating vehicles and fascinated spectators that clog the main surface artery from Detroit to Pontiac. Close to a million people line seven miles of Woodward Avenue on a mid-August Saturday to watch the passing show of 10,000 classic, collector and muscle cars; street rods; an unwelcome number of contemporary vehicles; and elaborate custom creations that have been — in the jargon of cruisers — channeled, chopped, Frenched, leaded, sectioned or tubbed.

(888) 493-2196   www.dreamcruise.org

MOST-SPECTACULAR AUTO RACE

DETROIT GRAND PRIX. Belle Isle.

For three days each June, Indy Car racing's biggest names power their 850 hp, turbocharged, aerodynamic, brightly colored, multimillion dollar machines around a world-class course laid out on America's largest urban island park.

(800) 498-7223   www.imgsports.com

MOST-POPULAR COLLECTOR-CAR SHOW

STRAITS AREA ANTIQUE AUTO SHOW. St. Ignace.

Each June more than 100,000 car buffs from all over North America descend on the tiny Straitside resort town of St. Ignace to ogle more than 3,000 unique classic and custom vehicles ranging from souped-up '50s Chevies to restored roadsters to $100,000 rarities. The 25-year-old, three-day-long event has been called both the "Woodstock" and "Mecca" of auto shows.

(800) 338-6660   www.st.ignace.com

COOLEST HOT-ROD EXHIBITION

DETROIT AUTORAMA.

For one weekend each winter, more than 800 hundred hot rods and wild custom cars, trucks, vans, and motorcycles are on display at America's first and biggest hot rod show.

(248) 650-5560

BEST NEW-CAR SHOW

NORTH AMERICAN INTERNATIONAL AUTO SHOW. Detroit.

Dazzling multimillion-dollar, high-tech displays that showcase more than 750 domestic and imported production-model and concept vehicles rank this annual extravaganza among the world's largest, most-spectacular and most-prestigious new-car exhibitions. The week-and-a-half-long event, held annually in early January, attracts a *Who's Who* of international automobile executives, nearly three quarters of a million tire-kicking visitors, and more journalists — 5,000, representing print, radio, television and on-line outlets around the globe — than any other North American show.

GOIN' SHOPPIN'
CAN'T STOP 'EM

CHOICEST PLACE TO SHOP FOR...

...ARCHITECTURAL ARTIFACTS

MATERIALS UNLIMITED. Ypsilanti.

A three-story red-brick building in downtown Ypsilanti holds one of the Midwest's largest and best collections of vintage architectural components, salvaged from abandoned and about-to-be-demolished buildings then refurbished and offered for sale.

The extraordinary, well-organized selection includes large numbers of the expected — ornate light fixtures, stained glass windows, French doors, mirrors, oak fireplace mantles, claw-foot tubs, pedestal sinks, and brass hinges, glass doorknobs, and other ornate hardware — plus the rare and unusual, such as a 500-pound stone carving of a medieval knight from the William Fisher mansion, an 8-foot-tall light fixture from Hudson's downtown department store, and the door to Henry Ford's office at the original Ford World Headquarters in Dearborn.

(800) 299-9462   www.materialsunlimited.com

...BEDDING PLANTS

EASTERN MARKET FLOWER DAY. Detroit.

On the Sunday after Mothers Day each year, more than 100,000 customers purchase 500,000 plants and flats and 50,000 shrubs and bushes at what's billed as the world's largest bedding plant market. Some 80 growers sell annuals, perennials, shrubs, evergreens and other plants at bargain prices at the 10-acre market, whose usual colorful atmosphere is made even more festive by clowns, singers, dancers, bands and other performers.

(313) 833-1560

...CARS, CLASSIC

CLASSIC AUTO SHOWPLACE. Madison Heights.

A continually changing, varied inventory of some 60-100 vehicles are displayed wheel to wheel in three connected showrooms at what is said to be the state's oldest and largest dealer of classic cars. For-sale lists at the consignment clearinghouse typically include lots of 1960s and '70s Camaros, Corvettes and Cutlasses plus a few unique dazzlers such as a $25,000 1973 DeTomaso Pantera, a $29,000 1958 silver Mercedes roadster, and a $33,000 black 1982 Ferrari.

(248) 589-2700   www.classicautoshowplace.com

...CARS, NEW

TROY MOTOR MALL. Troy.

Lined up uninterrupted along both sides of a single mile-long winding stretch of Maplelawn Road are Honda, Toyota, Volvo, Acura, Oldsmobile/Cadillac, Saab, Jaguar, Nissan, Saturn, Buick, Mazda, and Subaru new-car dealerships. And flanking them for about a mile along along Maple Road are huge Ford, Chrysler/Plymouth, Ford/Lincoln/Mercury, Chevrolet, and Pontiac/GMC outlets. The intense concentration is thought to be the world's largest concentration of auto showrooms.

...CHRISTMAS DECORATIONS

BRONNERS. Frankenmuth.

Filling an acre and a half of display space in the world's largest year-round Christmas store are 6,000 ornaments, 4,000 other trimmings, a forest of 260 different artificial trees, 500 styles of nativity scenes from 75 countries, 800 animated figures, and a staggering number of other decorations, collectibles, and gift items from around the globe.

(800) 255-9327   www.bronners.com

CHOICEST PLACE TO SHOP FOR...

...CLASSICAL MUSIC CD'S

SKR CLASSICAL. Ann Arbor.

With more than 20,000 titles, this UM campus-area store offers the state's greatest selection of classical compact disks, says *Hunts' Highlights of Michigan* (Midwestern Guides).

(800) 272-4506   www.skrclassical.com

...FOLK INSTRUMENTS AND MUSIC

ELDERLY INSTRUMENTS. Lansing.

This store and mail- and internet-order service is the nation's — some say the *world's* — best source of new and used folk instruments, instructional books, CDs, cassettes, and accessories. The huge, diverse inventory of instruments includes guitars, banjos, mandolins, ukuleles, fiddles, dulcimers, harmonicas, accordions, concertinas, bodhrans, resophonics, autoharps, and even washboards, musical saws, pennywhistles and kazoos. And one of four specialized Elderly catalogs is devoted to their vast multi- and cross-cultural selection of often-hard-to-find recorded folk music, from bluegrass to zydeco.

(517) 372-7890   www.elderly.com

...GOSPEL MUSIC

GOD'S WORLD. Detroit.

The selection of CDs, tapes, and records at this "gospel-artist clearinghouse" is so deep and wide that customers almost always find what they want in stock. If not, the owner— known as the "godfather of gospel music" — will order it.

(313) 862-8220

...HATS

HENRY THE HATTER. Detroit.

This legendary shop just northwest of Greektown has furnished politicians, entertainers, athletes, thousands of ordinary citizens, and even a few underworld figures with stylish headwear for more than a century. Stacked on shelves and perched on stands is "everything that's made," say the owners, including skullcaps, Stetsons, yacht caps, wool berets, Charlie Chan straw hats and British felt derbies.

(313) 962-0970

...HOCKEY EQUIPMENT

PERANI'S HOCKEY WORLD. Flint.

At 22,000 square feet, what may be the biggest hockey shop under one roof anywhere is filled with several thousand hockey sticks, shelves full of skates, a thousand pairs of goalie pads, and an exhaustive selection of other equipment for players in size down to the youngest mini-Mites and in price up to top-of-the-line professional models.

(800) 888-4625   www.peranis.com

...LODGEPOLE PINE FURNITURE

GREATER INDOORS. Birmingham.

This manufacturing and retail- and catalog-sales operation is one of the few sources nationwide for quality, contemporary, yet rustic pine furniture. The firm transforms lodgepole pine logs brought in from the foothills of the Rocky Mountains into custom-designed beds, dressers, nightstands, and other bedroom, living room and dining room furniture.

(800) 435-5647   www.americanlogfurniture.com

...MAGIC SUPPLIES

ABBOTTS MAGIC. Colon.

Available at the showroom of the world's largest manufacturer and supplier of magic equipment or from their 500-page catalog is a fascinating array of illusionists' hardware ranging from simple two-headed coins and folding top hats to a "head chopper" or a coffin-shaped box used to saw people in half.

(616) 432-3235   www.net-link.net/abbottmagic

...MARINE SUPPLIES

WOLF'S MARINE. Benton Harbor.

This 50,000-square-foot complex holds what is claimed to be the Midwest's largest and most-varied inventory of supplies, parts (including hard-to-find replacements) and accessories for owners of floating craft from rubber rafts to maxi yachts. Tens of thousands of items include, to name just a few, anchors, horns, compasses, books and charts, apparel, trailers and supplies, lighting and fixtures, chrome and brass hardware, toilets, electronics, seats, carpeting, and rope ranging in diameter from little-finger to leg-size.

(616) 926-1068   www.wolfsmarine.com

CHOICEST PLACE TO SHOP FOR...

...OUTDOOR ADORNMENTS

KRUPP'S NOVELTY SHOP. Lennon.

This block-square complex holds the state's largest and most-varied assortment of decorations for yard, garden and anywhere-else outdoors. The selection — from kitsch to classic and miniature to larger-than-life — includes several thousand fountains, bird baths, swings, picnic tables, garden benches, gazebos, children's playcenters, wishing wells, windmills, pottery, trellises, arbors, patio stones, and a tremendous number and variety of religious, animal and other statuaries.

(810) 621-3752
www.krupps.com

...PIPES

PAUL'S PIPE SHOP. Flint.

More than a million pipes, ranging from inexpensive corncobs to a $5,000 Dunhill, are for sale at this 50-year-old downtown shop, the state's and perhaps Midwest's largest purveyor of pipes. The owner, a six-time world pipe-smoking champion, also custom blends tobacco, is the curator of a second-floor pipe museum, and has become nationally known for making difficult pipe repairs.

(810) 235-0581

...QUILTING SUPPLIES

COUNTRY STITCHES. Lansing.

Michigan's — likely the country's — largest quilt shop offers a tremendous selection of everything needed by people who painstakingly piece patches. The huge corner strip-mall complex encloses 6,000 bolts of fabrics, hundreds of books and patterns, 30 styles of rulers, threads, needles, thimbles, sewing machines, and useful gadgets, gift items and supplies, plus four classrooms used by beginning through advanced quilting students.

(800) 572-2031   www.countrystitches.com

...SHOES, EXOTIC

CITY SLICKER SHOES. Detroit.

Bold, colorful alligator and snakeskin footwear, once worn only by street hustlers and entertainers, has gone mainstream out of this corner shop just west of Greektown. More than two dozen different vivid colors — such as electric blue, hot pink, and neon lime green — are splashed in striking mix-and-match patterns on styles from wing tips to thigh-high boots. The resulting 150 color/style combinations is said to be the world's largest selection of exotic skin shoes.

(313) 963-1963

...USED BOOKS

JOHN KING BOOKS. Detroit.

With nearly a million rare and used volumes neatly organized on hundreds of shelves that fill a 30,000-square-foot, four-story former glove factory, this legendary store ranks among the nation's largest and best of its kind.

BEST RESORTS TO RESORT TO GO SHOPPING

PETOSKEY.

The casually upscale area of downtown Petoskey known as the Gaslight District is made up of an unmatched blend of nearly 80 non-chain, individualistic retailers — including boutiques, galleries, two outstanding independent bookstores, eclectic gift and specialty shops, gourmet food outlets, and apparel (particularly resort and/or ski wear) and shoe stores — many housed in Victorian brick-fronted buildings.

(800) 845-2828   www.boynecountry.com

SAUGATUCK.

The half-square-mile downtown area of this tiny, scenic resort village comprises Michigan's most-concentrated yet wildly varied collection of unique gift shops, trendy boutiques, and two dozen quality artists' galleries and studios.

(616) 857-5801   www.saugatuck.com

TONIEST MALL

SOMERSET COLLECTION. Troy.

The Somerset Collection in Troy offers Michigan's most-upscale and -exclusive shopping experience. Among 180 stores are such distinguished Miracle Mile and New York Fifth Avenue merchants as Neiman Marcus, Saks, Gucci, Tiffany & Co. and Crate & Barrel. And more than a third of the distinctive shops — Louis Vuitton, Pottery Barn, and Restoration Hardware, for examples — are the only ones of their kind in Michigan.

(248) 643-6360

LARGEST STANDARD-ISSUE MALL

TWELVE OAKS. Novi.

Michigan's "megamall" encloses 190 stores, more than any other of the state's conventional, suburban shopping malls.

(248) 348-9400

BEST PLACE TO MIX SHOPPING WITH PLEASURE

or if shopping to you *is* pleasure, then

DOUBLE YOUR PLEASURE, DOUBLE YOUR FUN

GREAT LAKES CROSSING. Auburn Hills.

Michigan's newest, largest and first-of-its-kind complex is a high-energy mix of interactive "value" shopping and high-tech entertainment, a blend of Saks and Speilberg, Disney and Donna Karan in a 1½-million-square-foot enclosed area. Nearly 200 stores include upscale factory outlets such as Neiman Marcus Last Call, Saks Off Fifth, and Bernini "Off Rodeo" and specialty stores such as Bass Pro Outdoor World. Many retailers sell their wares out of themed settings, including places to test out merchandise before buying. Anglers, for instance, toss lures into an indoor river, in-line skaters race around a track, and golfers swing clubs on five different simulated courses.

Nonshoppers head for the 35,000-square-foot GameWorks area (p. 4), a $2 million indoor children's playground, the state's largest movie megaplex (p. 5), a brew pub, or the Rain Forest Cafe, complete with live birds, talking trees, waterfalls and an occasional tropical storm that rolls through.

(248) 454-5000   www.greatlakescrossing.com

LARGEST OUTLET MALL

OUTLETS AT BIRCH RUN. Birch Run.

A maze of eight interconnected and almost-connected strip malls just off I-75 makes up one of the country's largest factory-direct retail centers. More than 170 manufacturer-owned outlets fill 1.4 million square feet of sales area with a wide range of products at discount prices.

(517) 624-7467   www.horizongroup.com

MOST-UNIQUE FACTORY OUTLET

MARQUETTE STATE PRISON GIFT SHOP. Marquette.

Inmates supply this small shop's entire inventory, "prison hobby craft" that you won't find at any other store anywhere. Yellow price tags on the leather products, paintings, handmade fishing flies, polished-stone jewelry and other items are marked with the identification numbers of their creators, who receive the money if and when released.

(800) 544-4321

BIGGEST FLEA MARKETS

GIBRALTAR TRADE CENTERS. Taylor and Mt. Clemens.

Each year more than four million bargain hunters descend upon these two huge, lively indoor/outdoor weekend markets to haggle with hundreds of vendors offering just about every kind of new and used merchandise imaginable at cut-rate, negotiable prices.

(734) 287-2000   (810) 465-6440   www.gibraltartrade.com

MOST-UPSCALE ANTIQUES SHOW

GREENFIELD VILLAGE ANTIQUES SHOW. Dearborn.

This annual May weekend-long affair is promoted as the "creme de la creme" of Michigan's plethora of antique shows, malls, markets, centers and shops. Forty "pedigreed dealers" offering predominantly museum-quality merchandise make this the state's "priciest" venue, claim the organizers, who also offer an opportunity to "rub elbows with the area's rich and famous" at a $350-per-ticket Preview Party.

(313) 982-6044

MOST-PRESTIGIOUS ANTIQUES MARKET

(Margaret Brusher's)

ANN ARBOR ANTIQUES MARKET. Ann Arbor.

Many dedicated antiquers rate this more than 30-year-old show — held the third Sunday of the month each May through November — as the best in the Midwest. The more than 300 dealers are screened for quality, they aren't allowed to do other area shows, and their good-to-fine merchandise is guaranteed.

(734) 662-9453

PALATE PLEASERS

BEST VIRTUAL TO REAL-TIME PASTIES

PASTY CENTRAL. Calumet.

In a unique union of tradition and technology, residents and staff of the Still Waters Community Elders Home in remote Keweenaw County hand-make pasties — Cornish-origin, dough-wrapped blends of meats and vegetables — which they then market on the Internet for home delivery anywhere in the country. Each month 20-25 assisted-living seniors — average age 84 and with 1,000 years of combined pasty-making experience — help masterfully prepare, bake, freeze and ship some 800 portions of the Copper Country's "official food."

www.pasty.com

MOST-POPULAR U.P. TOASTER

TRENARY HOME BAKERY. Trenary.

After pasties, the next best-loved U.P. food may be Finnish *korpu,* a slightly sweet, toasted bread sprinkled with cinnamon, sugar and spices and then slowly baked. And its prime purveyor is the Trenary Home Bakery, which bakes, distributes and sells so many pieces — more than 40,000 weekly, packaged in 12-ounce brown paper bags — that the coffee-dunking treat is known throughout the U.P. as "Trenary Toast."

(800) 862-7801

LARGEST SWEET ROLLS

HILLTOP RESTAURANT. L'Anse.

Available warm and flaky on site or frozen via UPS from this family-owned restaurant at the tip of Keweenaw Bay are the state's hugest home-made sweet rolls — one-pound, six-inch-in-diameter, 3-inch thick, apple-infused, cinnamon-spiced, sugar-glazed diet busters.

(906) 524-7858   www.sweetroll.com

FRESHEST MAIL-ORDER WHITEFISH

MACKINAC STRAITS FISH COMPANY. St. Ignace.

Whitefish in the smoked fillets, sausages and spreads from this small processor practically jump from the water into vacuum-sealed packaging. Harvested from the cold Straits just steps away and only after orders are received, the fish are hand-selected, cut to exacting specifications, smoked within 24 hours and shipped ready-to-eat from the package.

(888) 333-1823

MOST-HIGHLY ACCLAIMED PURVEYOR OF FINE FRUIT PRODUCTS

AMERICAN SPOON FOODS. Petoskey.

American Spoon Foods has earned national and international awards, recognition and lofty status by developing and perfecting a field-to-table process that captures, concentrates and preserves the natural flavor of select, superb Northern Michigan-grown fruits. Their ever-expanding line of what some say are the world's finest fruit products includes lengthy lists of dried fruits, toppings, butters, relishes, sauces, jellies, jams and preserves.

(800) 222-5886   www.spoon.com

MOST SPIRITUAL FRUIT

THE JAMPOT. Eagle River.

As part of their reflective routine, Society of St. John monks harvest wild Keweenaw-area thimble-berries, blackberries, cherries, boysenberries, choke-cherries, crabapples, pincherries, bilberries, strawberries, dewberries, currants, raspberries, rhubarb, plums, blueberries and cranberries and turn them into a tremendous variety of Poorrock Abbey-brand jams, jellies, butters, marmalades and other conserves and preserves, which they sell on site and by mail, FAX, or email, but not phone.

www.societystjohn.com
(e-mail) skete@societystjohn.com
(FAX) 906-289-4388

MOST HISTORIC MAIL-ORDER APPLES

KILCHERMAN'S CHRISTMAS COVE FARM. Northport.

Nearly 200 varieties of antique, rare and little-known foreign and domestic apples grow on more than 3,000 trees at this 85-acre Leelanau Peninsula family-run orchard. Among the unique, fascinating specimens are the Green Newton Pippin, a tart apple from 1722 that is considered America's oldest; the Spitzenburg, an orange fruit with gray spots that was favored by Thomas Jefferson; and the Lady Apple, which 17th-century French women used as a breath freshener.

Twelve- and 16-count sampler boxes, available at the farm and by mail-order, come with printed historical facts and anecdotes for each of the included fruits.

(231) 386-5637   www.traverse.net/christmascove

TASTIEST FUNGUS

MOREL MUSHROOM.

North America's tastiest, most-popular and most-expensive wild mushroom grows throughout Michigan. During the fungi's late-spring growing season, thousands of gourmands search Michigan's woods for the elusive, distinctive-looking and -tasting delicacy that, in stores, costs $150-250 per pound for dried whole specimens.

CHOICEST PLACE TO ADD SPICE TO YOUR LIFE

RAFAL SPICE. Detroit.

Arranged alphabetically on shelves that line the walls of this small, fragrant Eastern Market shop are 5-pound glass canisters holding more than 400 herbs and spices, including more than 40 different kinds of pepper and dozens of special blends for use in preparing foods from soups to sausages.

(313) 259-6373

RAREST SAUSAGE STUFFER

ZICK'S SPECIALTY MEATS AND SAUSAGES. Berrien Springs.

Each week, workers at this small, family-operated shop grind, shape, smoke and otherwise process some 2½ tons of ostrich, alligator, kangaroo, buffalo and other exotic and wild-game meats into sausage links and jerky strips, most for other companies that package and sell millions of the meat snacks under their own labels.

(616) 471-7121

LARGEST NATURAL-PRODUCTS RETAILER

APPLE VALLEY MARKET. Berrien Springs.

Those who prefer or require a life devoid of meat, preservatives, sugar, salt, glutin, chemical additives, or anything else considered unhealthy have more choices at this large, unique complex than anywhere else in the state. Several thousand products are stacked in deli-style coolers and freezers and on what appears to be miles of shelving.

"Natural" replacements are available for just about every food product imaginable, including an amazing array of soya vegetable protein substitutes for fried chicken, ocean fillets, salami and other meats. Arranged alphabetically are nearly 100 different herbal teas and just as many "natural" alternatives to manmade pharmaceuticals.

And a long and fascinating list of non-food products made from naturally occurring compounds includes lichen-based deodorants.

(616) 471-3234

BEST INVENTED-IN-MICHIGAN BEVERAGES

VERNORS.

Detroit pharmacist James Vernor concocted the recipe for the nation's oldest soft drink in 1866.

ICE CREAM SODAS.

When on a hot day in 1875 a harried clerk for the Sanders Store in Detroit ran out of the sweet cream normally used to make sodas, he substituted ice cream, and the new treat became a Sander's specialty for the next two decades.

FRESHEST TAP INTO MICHIGAN-MADE BEER

MICHIGAN BEER GUIDE
WWW.MICHIGANBEERGUIDE.COM

This 24-page monthly newsletter and companion website are excellent ways to keep track of Michigan's burgeoning breweries, brewpubs and microbreweries. Regular features include articles on new openings, updates on established sites, interviews with brewers and chefs (sometimes including recipes), how-to's on the art and science of beer and beermaking, and a current directory, including locator map and beer list, for all 65 (and growing) Michigan establishments serving "craft-brewed" beers.

P.O. Box 648, Leonard, MI 48367-1635   (248) 628-6584

BEST WINE SHOP

VILLAGE CORNER. Ann Arbor.

This unpretentious oenophile haven (some say heaven) just off the University of Michigan campus advertises itself not only as having Michigan's largest wine selection — 4,000, including 100 from Michigan — but also the state's most-knowledgeable wine staff and most-informative wine catalog. The *Pocket Guide to Detroit & Michigan Restaurants* (Momentum Books Ltd.) agrees, saying that the 30-year-old store is "one of the most respected wine shops in the Midwest...(with)...good prices and a spectacular range," and that the regularly issued free catalogs "are wine courses in themselves."

(734) 995-1818   www.villagecorner.com

MOST-RENOWNED DELI

ZINGERMAN'S DELI. Ann Arbor.

For nearly 20 years, legendary Zingerman's has ranked with and, in one important aspect, better than nationally known New York delis. Their Kerrytown complex offers an outstanding selection of some 3,000 domestic and international gourmet and specialty foods; a lengthy, wide-ranging list of take-out items; and a choice of nearly 100 varieties of large sandwiches made with flavorful bread made at the Zingerman Bakehouse. And unlike their eastern big-city counterparts, Zingerman's knowledgeable staff has earned a reputation for being consistently professional, polite and patient.

(888) 636-8162   www.zingermans.com

MOST-PRODIGIOUS PLANT MILKER

EDEN FOODS CO. (Clinton) operates North America's largest soy-milk processing and packaging plant, and their Edensoy is the country's best-selling brand of the low-fat dietary substitute.

(517) 456-7424

GREATEST GOURMET GROCER

VIC'S WORLD CLASS MARKET. Novi.

Designed to resemble a European town square, this $10 million, 89,000-square-foot "food emporium" includes a greenhouse, floral area, deli, wine cellar, butcher shop, bakery, seafood shop, soda fountain, and milk bar and stocks more than 10,000 gourmet food products; produce, including exotic mushrooms, edible flowers and tropical fruits; and ready-to-eat items such as caper and anchovy stuffed peppers and a sushi-roll selection.

(248) 305-7333

MOST-UPSCALE LARGE-CHAIN GROCERY STORE

FARMER JACK FOOD EMPORIUM. Grosse Pointe Woods.

This $12 million outlet opened in 1998 complete with a sushi bar, wine steward, grilled-chicken Caesar salad station and full-service panini sandwich bar. Other items and services not usually found in standard-issue chain outlets include gourmet take-out meals prepared by a caterer, 30 different microbrews that can be mixed to make up sampler six packs, a commissioned mural, and cakes that can be custom-topped by a computer that turns photographs into edible frosting.

BEST BIATHLON BUFFETS

GOURMET GLIDES. Garland Resort, Lewiston.

During these winter-weekend progressive dinners, cross-country skiers follow a 10K course that includes stops at five trailside buffets serving wild-game sausage, fruit fondue, smoked lake trout, carved smoked rounds of beef, pheasant and other gourmet dishes.

(800) 968-0042   www.garlandusa.com

RECORD-SETTING SERVINGS

CHICKEN BARBEQUE. Manchester.

For four hours on the third Thursday of each July, 550 volunteers serve a ton of cole slaw, 950 dozen rolls, and 6,000 butter-basted, barbequed chickens to 10,000-12,000 outdoor diners at Michigan's largest chicken barbeque.

(734) 428-7877

WORLD'S LARGEST PIE. Charlevoix.

To help celebrate the nation's bicentennial, Charlevoix residents baked a 7-ton cherry pie that measured 14 feet, 4 inches in diameter, was 24 inches deep, and contained nearly 2½ tons of cherries.

WORLD'S LARGEST CHERRY PIE	
5,850 lbs	Red Tart Cherries
3,850 "	Cherry Juice
4,750 "	Sugar
740 "	Cornstarch
360 "	Tapioca
180 "	Butter
90 "	Lemon Juice
20 "	Salt
750 "	Flour
325 "	Shortning
325 "	Water
110 "	Milk
55 "	Baking Powder
15 "	Salt

CRUST

WORLD'S LARGEST SUBMARINE SANDWICH. Flint.

During the 1982 Fourth of July celebration, a Flint area grocery store chain prepared and served a 1,000-foot-long bun stuffed with 2,600 slices of cheese; 3,300 slices of lunchmeat; 25 pounds of mustard; ½ ton of shredded lettuce; and 100 pounds of chopped onions.

Aarhvirk Studio
Flint Journal

RECORD-SETTING SERVINGS

WORLD'S LARGEST BREAKFAST. Battle Creek.

Each June the Cereal City competes with Springfield, Massachusetts, to see which can serve the world's largest breakfast, measured by the number of people served. By consistently handing out more than 60,000 six-course breakfasts — cereal, milk, a donut hole, a Pop Tart, a banana and Tang — to people who then sit at several hundred tables lining its downtown streets, Battle Creek usually wins.

(800) 397-2240   www.battlecreekvisitors.org

WORLD'S LARGEST PASTY BAKE. St. Ignace.

On Sunday of each Memorial Day weekend the Paul Bunyan Restaurant bakes a 200-pound version of the U.P.'s best-known dish, then hands out free slices of it plus a soft drink to the first 150 people who stop by.

(800) 338-6660   www.stignace.com

TOP-RATED RESTAURANT

We Michiganians have extraordinary opportunities to dine at hundreds of outstanding restaurants, including a dozen or so that rank as national-destination and world-class. And the standout among the standouts is

THE LARK. West Bloomfield.

The state's most-honored *haute* dining establishment has received #1-in-the-state ratings from just about every respected critic and reviewer. It is also the "people's choice," having been voted the favorite of *Zagat Survey* respondents and *Gourmet* magazine readers. And in 1995 it was even named the best restaurant in the *country* by *Condé Nast Traveler* subscribers. A rustic, relaxing Portuguese country-inn decor; a creative, eclectic new-French menu; delectable, beautifully presented plates; an outstanding wine list; and consistent, superb service from long-time employees are reasons the Lark has earned and maintained its lofty reputation.

(248) 661-4466

FINEST UP-NORTH RESTAURANT

TAPAWINGO. Ellsworth.

Presentation at the Tapawingo is so artistic that some patrons have photographed their entrees, which is one reason why this resort-area restaurant rivals and sometimes beats the urban Lark for best-in-the-state honors. Tapawingo's menu of superbly prepared new-American food emphasizes the innovative use of Michigan-grown ingredients, and their awards-winning wine selection lists 850 vintages. All is expertly served at an elegant former summer residence on the shore of a small lake.

(231) 588-7971

TRAVELER'S CHECKS

TOP-FIVE REASONS TO GO TO

a rural Livingston County community, pop. 340 Hellions.

1. To say you've been there and back.
2. In summer, to see if your home town is hotter than Hell.
3. In winter, to see if Hell has frozen over.
4. To buy a souvenir such as a tiny (baseball) bat out of Hell.
5. To get a letter or card hand-stamped with a mailed-from-Hell postmark.

CHOICEST ROUTES TO FABULOUS FALL COLOR

More than half of Michigan is forest land, 75% of which is covered with hardwoods whose foliage turns to brilliant autumn reds, yellows and oranges. With so many billions of leaves, it's not always easy to decide where and when to soak up peak displays of stunning color.

The most-comprehensive help comes from the Michigan Jobs Commission, Travel Michigan whose *Fall Calendar of Events* booklet charts usual peak color times throughout the state and also suggests more than two dozen outstanding, diverse color drives. You can also call them at (800) 644-3255 in season and (888) 784-7328 year-round or check their web site, www.michigan.org, for regularly updated color conditions.

EASIEST COUNTY TO COMMUTE

LAKE is the only Michigan county where motorists can travel every mile of roadway, including US-10 and M-37, without encountering a single red-yellow-green traffic signal.

MOST-CREATIVE EXCUSES FOR SPEEDING

Most motorists who have been pulled over for exceeding posted speed limits try avoiding a citation by blurting out hopelessly unimaginative and redundant excuses, such as

- I have to go to the bathroom (the hands-down, number-one excuse).
- I'm late for work.
- My speedometer must be off.
- I didn't see the speed limit signs.
- I was just going with the flow.
- The wind must have blown me over the limit.
- I have to hurry to the gas station before I run out of fuel.

To possibly avoid getting a ticket if stopped, try to be more original, such as

- the man and his wife, both wearing crash helmets, who said they had to rush home to their basement to take shelter from an oncoming tornado.
- the man who pleaded, "Officer, my wife is going to get pregnant tonight, and I want to be there when she does."

MOST-COMPLETE GUIDE TO FAMILY FUN

KIDS CATALOG OF MICHIGAN ADVENTURES
(Wayne State University Press) by Ellyce Field

Anyone who has to or wants to keep children entertained and stimulated should hug this regularly updated guide, which features essential, up-to-date details — like location, hours, admission, age appeal, parking and facilities — and brief descriptions for more than 2,000 kid-friendly destinations and diversions. The wide range of year-round, state-wide excursions includes birthday party locations, tours, youth theaters, horseback riding, museums, historic sites, zoos, nature centers, parks, beaches, u-pick farms, sports, and airplane, boat, train, trolley and tram rides, to name just a few.

MUST-HAVE, GO-TO GUIDES

HUNTS' ESSENTIAL MICHIGAN: LOWER PENINSULA
(formerly *Hunt's Highlights of Michigan*)
HUNTS' GUIDE TO MICHIGAN'S UPPER PENINSULA
(Midwestern Guides) by Don and Mary Hunt

Using these two phenomenal guides is like having a friend in any conceivable area of the state — big city, country or isolated corner — who can tell you in exhaustive detail what there is interesting to see or do, particularly those "ins" and "avoids" best known only to locals. Because of their incredibly thorough research and uncanny insight, the authors come across as knowledgeable lifetime residents of everywhere Michigan. And like good locals, they both emphasize and honestly evaluate otherwise less-well-publicized attractions and nonchain restaurants and lodging.

LARGEST RV SHOW

PONTIAC SILVERDOME
CAMPER, TRAVEL & RV SHOW. Pontiac.
For five days in late January each year, the world's largest air-supported roof covers several hundred different models of new motor homes, travel trailers, tent campers, fifth wheels, tow vehicles plus accessories and just about anything else RV related. On-site financing is available, and representatives from public and private campgrounds are on hand to try to steer RV owners their way.
(616) 530-1919

HIGHEST-RATED HOTELS

Only three Michigan hotels consistently earn all of these respected, prestigious top ratings: Four Diamond (AAA), Gold (*Condé Nast Traveler*), and Four Star (*Mobile Travel Guide*). They are the

AMWAY GRAND. Grand Rapids
(800) 253-3590   www.amwaygrand.com

RITZ CARLTON. Dearborn
(800) 241-3333

TOWNSEND. Birmingham
(800) 548-4172

The three rank among world-class luxury lodgings because they consistently provide exceptional hospitality, including twice-daily maid and 24-hour room services; amenities such as Belgian linens, 200 thread-count pressed sheets, luxury soap and fresh-cut flowers; skilled, professional staff, such as the Townsend's concierge who speaks seven languages and the Ritz Carlton's afternoon doorman, rated the country's best; and elegant, spacious facilities lavishly appointed with wood paneling, marble, crystal chandeliers, pricey antiques, rich fabrics and museum-quality art.

MOST-SPECTACULAR CONDOMINIUM HOTEL

THE INN AT BAY HARBOR. Bay Harbor.
At this stunning, new 175,000 square-foot Victorian-style, 130-room resort hotel overlooking Little Traverse Bay, private individuals can purchase a one-, two- or three-bedroom luxury suite and then, when not using it, recoup a portion of the several-hundred-thousand-dollar cost by renting the accommodations to the public. Owners and overnight guests can make full use of the $20 million facility's full range of services, including a private beach along 1,000 feet of shoreline, a first-class lake-front restaurant with indoor and outdoor dining, a world-class spa and health club, a free-form pool, a croquet lawn and a putting course.
(231) 439-4000   www.bayharbor.com

GRANDEST SUMMER RESORT HOTEL

THE GRAND. Mackinac Island.

The world's largest and oldest resort hotel also ranks among the world's best and for good reason. Guests at the stark-white, pillared wood behemoth are time-warped into an elegant Victorian-era experience that includes distinctly decorated, radioless, TV-less rooms; six-course gourmet dinners served by tuxedoed, white-gloved waiters; demitasse and High Tea accompanied by chamber music; horse-drawn carriages driven by top-hatted coachmen; the world's longest and most-photographed front porch; outstanding views of the Straits of Mackinac and Mackinac Bridge; and 500 acres of meticulously maintained grounds lush with more than 100,00 annuals, perennials and wildflowers.

(800) 334-7263   www.grandhotel.com

GRANDEST VINTAGE LOG LODGE

KEWEENAW MOUNTAIN RESORT. Copper Harbor.

CUSHIEST CAT HOUSE

BACKDOOR FRIENDS. Farmington Hills.

Cat-owning travelers can board their pets in unaccustomed style at this 16-room luxury feline facility. Each of the 6- by 6-foot rooms is fitted with three levels of perches and cubby holes and is theme decorated. A Victorian Suite, for instance, is furnished with a hardwood-rail bed and decorated with 18th-century artwork. And a Geriatric Room for older cats is equipped with ramps leading up to perches and windowsills. All guests are indulged with room-service meals and individually scheduled daily exercise time in a large, toy-filled playscape area.

(248) 442-0840

TOP-RATED RESORT

GARLAND. Lewiston.

Golfers and cross-country skiers can enjoy their pastimes in unmatched, secluded, scenic, rustic luxury at the Midwest's only AAA-rated Four Diamond year-round resort. Indulgences include four championship golf courses, immaculately groomed ski trails that cut through 3,500 wooded acres, formal and casual fine dining, and overnight accommodations — with marble baths, jacuzzis and gas-log fireplaces — in either the largest log lodge east of the Mississippi or a private villa or cottage.

(800) 968-0042   www.garlandusa.com

Using white pines cut to clear land for a nine-hole golf course, unemployed Depression-era miners constructed this huge rustic log lodge and 23 suite-type log cabins plus the furniture to fill them. An enormous stone fireplace fronts the lodge's dining area, another warms a lounge, and all of the original cabins come with their own fireplaces as well. And also as at the western national park complexes they mimicked, the public-works-funded structures here feature porches and lots of steeply pitched gabled roofs.

(906) 289-4403   www.portup.com/~lodge/

CHOICEST BED-AND-BREAKFAST CITY

SAUGATUCK.

This small, distinctive resort community includes more than 30 bed-and-breakfasts, the highest concentration of any city in the state according to AAA's *Michigan Living* magazine. The overnight accommodations range from historic mansions to renovated boathouses.

(616) 857-5801   www.saugatuck.com

BEST RESORT RANCH

DOUBLE JJ. Rothbury.

Michigan's premier "dude ranch" serves up a unique and unmatched blend of adult and family, western and city-slicker facilities, activities and entertainment. Lodging includes an adults-only ranch house, family cabins or upscale hotel rooms, and parents may overnight their kids, under staff supervision, in Conestoga wagons, tree houses, tepees or bunk houses. Horseback rides geared to experience, rodeos, and country line-dancing are on the long list of Western-style activities for cowboy wanna-be's over 18. The saddle-weary and -wary make their way to an 18-hole championship golf course; archery and rifle ranges; cross-country ski trails; tennis and volleyball courts; a heated swimming pool and outdoor hot tub; a private lake with beach, paddleboats, rowboats and canoes; or the Sundance Saloon and Steakhouse, where nightly entertainment includes live bands, DJs, karaoke and stage shows.

The Back Forty — a supervised kids-only resort within the resort — has its own equestrian area, plus a "swimmin' hole" with a 145-foot water slide and rope swings, crafts barns, a petting farm and an Old West town, where holdups and corral showdowns are staged.

(800) 368-2535   www.doublejj.com

Double JJ Resort

RAREST NIGHT LIGHTS

Of the mere half dozen lighthouses in the nation that take in overnight guests, two are in the Upper Peninsula.

BIG BAY POINT LIGHTHOUSE. Big Bay.

This solid century-old red brick structure perches near the edge of a cliff that drops 50 feet to the rocky Lake Superior shore. Guests who climb to the top of the light tower get great views of the world's second-largest freshwater lake and rugged surrounding countryside.

(906) 345-9957   www.lighthousebandb.com

SAND HILLS LIGHTHOUSE. Ahmeek.

Guests at this imposing brick lighthouse "have a rare opportunity to step into the world of a late-18th century lightkeeper," says *A Traveler's Guide to 116 Michigan Lighthouses* (Friede Publications). Eight bedrooms have been refurbished and furnished with antiques to look as they did when lightkeepers and their families worked and lived here from 1919 to 1939.

(906) 337-1744   www.sandhillslighthouseinn.com

BEST FLOATING BED-AND-BREAKFAST

Traverse Tall Ship Co.

MALABAR. Traverse City.

A 2½-hour sunset sail followed by an overnight pierside stay aboard this 105-foot-long replica of a mid-1800s "tall ship" gives a realistic taste of early 19th-century sailing. Guests crawl into rustic wood bunks in closet-size compartments, share a head (bathroom), and take showers on shore, but wake to what may be the largest, heartiest morning meal served at any Michigan bed and breakfast.

(231) 941-2000 www.tallshipsailing.com

BEST ENGINEERED OVERNIGHT ACCOMMODATION

COE RAIL. Walled Lake.

Passengers who climb aboard the nation's first bed-and-breakfast train temporarily time warp to a 1950s rail travel experience that includes a five-course gourmet dinner, live entertainment, and overnight accommodations in a classic plush Pullman sleeper car.

(248) 960-9440 www.michiganstarclipper.com

BEST PLACE TO SIP AND SLEEP

CHATEAU CHANTAL. Traverse City.

Perched like a castle on an Old Mission Peninsula hilltop with outstanding views of both East and West Grand Traverse bays, Chateau Chantal is the only winery in the state that offers bed-and-breakfast accommodations. Before retiring to suites with sitting rooms and private baths, overnight guests sample the winery's vintages in a huge, elegant tasting room that includes a polished-granite-topped bar, fireplace, baby-grand piano and wide bay window overlooking the bays.

(800) 969-4009 www.chateauchantal.com

GRANDEST VINTAGE WILDERNESS CAMP

MICHIGAMME LAKE LODGE. Champion.

Built by unemployed Depression-era miners for a wealthy businessman/financier, this huge Adirondack-style summer home atop a bluff overlooking Lake Michigamme was constructed with local white pine logs and quarried stone.

Since 1988 the beautiful lodge has operated as a bed-and-breakfast inn whose owners have maintained its original rustic character. Inside, a pair of hand-hewn stairways rise to twin balconies that overlook a great room dominated by an immense 2½-story stone fireplace and lighted by unique, electrified cedar-stump chandeliers. Antique tools, decoys, deer heads and bearskins adorn the exposed log interior walls; original custom-made bird's-eye maple furniture is used in nine large guest rooms; and original Adirondack and twig furniture is spread along a 40-foot sun porch.

(906) 632-3311

INTO THE GREAT WIDE OPEN

PEAK VIEWS

COPPER PEAK. Bessemer.

A chairlift ride to the crest of 800-foot-high Copper Peak followed by an elevator lift and stair climb up another 26 stories end at the top of the world's highest manmade ski jump, with sweeping views out over Lake Superior to Wisconsin's Apostle Islands, the Arrowhead region of Minnesota and Thunder Bay, Canada and inland over thousands of acres of Michigan's Ottawa National Forest.

(906) 932-3500

SUMMIT PEAK. Porcupine Mountains State Park.

A 40-foot-tall observation tower jutting up from the highest point (1,958 feet) in Michigan's largest state park offers unmatched looks over the lakes, waterfalls, rivers, mountains, forests and Lake Superior coastline of the 60,000-acre park itself plus distant glimpses of Wisconsin, Minnesota and the Apostle Islands.

(906) 885-5275

SUPERIOR PANORAMA

MISSION HILL. Brimley.

A well-marked turnoff from Lakeshore Drive five miles west of M-221 winds up to an overlook, visited mostly only by locals, with a spectacular, sweeping view over Spectacle Lake and across Lake Superior to Canada. Poking up out of the pines and hardwoods to the left (north) is the lantern room of Pt. Iroquois Lighthouse, and after leaves drop in fall, or in summer if you follow a trail to the right (south), the panorama also takes in Monocole Lake.

TOP-NOTCH DRIVE

BROCKWAY MOUNTAIN DRIVE. Copper Harbor.

"Number-one scenic drive in the state" and "most scenic public drive in the Midwest" are phrases routinely used to describe the highest above-sea-level (1,337 feet) roadway between the Appalachians and Rockies. On clear days from the crest of the 9.5-mile route, you can look out 50 miles over Lake Superior to Isle Royale. To the south the view over the edge of a 300-foot-high cliff can be better than bird's-eye; during hawk migration you can look *down* on the soaring birds.

(906) 482-2388

MOST-PHOTOGRAPHED LOOKED-DOWN-UPON SCENES

LAKE OF THE CLOUDS. Porcupine Mountains State Park. ▲

MINERS CASTLE. Pictured Rocks National Lakeshore. ▶

MOST-UNIQUELY BEAUTIFUL BIRDS-EYE VIEW

Unmatched, spectacular views of Sleeping Bear Dunes, Lake Michigan, Crystal Lake, the Betsie River, Betsie Lake and the twin ports of Frankfort and Elberta come from 2,000-3,000 feet up during a ride in a small two-seat glider piloted by a certified member of Frankfort's Northwest Soaring Club. The inexpensive, thrilling tow, float and drop — available by phone appointment from May to October — lasts from 30 minutes to a couple of hours depending on the prevalence or lack of thermal updrafts called "bumps."

(616) 352-9160

RAREST TIED-DOWN, UP-IN-THE-AIR VIEW

VIRGIN SKYRIDES. Birch Run.

The nation's first Old World-style tethered balloon ride launches amateur aeronauts 500 feet into the air for a 5-minute view over the surrounding countryside including Frankenmuth, the Saginaw River nearly to its mouth, and downtowns Flint, Saginaw and Bay City. Anchored to the ground by a 2-inch steel cable, the 100-foot-tall balloon can safely lift an attached, enclosed 30-passenger gondola in winds up to 25 mph and at night.

(517) 624-5355

HIGHEST URBAN PANORAMA

MARRIOTT HOTEL. Renaissance Center, Detroit.

Rising up 73 floors (748 feet) from street level, the gleaming tower centering the Renaissance Center is the world's tallest hotel and Michigan's tallest building. The sweeping view from its circular, glass-paneled observation level offers a one-of-a-kind perspective of the state's largest city and beyond — up the Detroit River past Belle Isle to Lake St. Clair and downriver over the Ambassador Bridge almost to Lake Erie.

(313) 568-8000

MOST-REWARDING LONG STAIR CLIMBS

AVALANCHE OVERLOOK. Boyne City.

Four hundred fifty-one steps up the face of Bald Mountain lead to what some rate as the Lower Peninsula's most-scenic high point. From an observation platform on the summit you look down on a beautiful, colorful, living map of Boyne City, the north arm of Lake Charlevoix, and surrounding hills.

(231) 582-6222

DUNE OVERLOOK. Hoffmaster State Park, Muskegon.

Nearly 200 steps rise up 180 feet through a thick, mature beech-maple forest to a platform offering one of the Lake Michigan dune area's most-spectacularly panoramic perspectives.

(231) 798-3573

MOST SURREAL LOOK AT THE WINDY CITY

WARREN DUNES STATE PARK. Bridgman.

On clear days from the faces and summits of Pikes Peak and Tower Hill sand dunes you can see Chicago 50 miles across Lake Michigan. As you climb up the sand mountains, the Sears Tower, Hancock Building, and other skyline features correspondingly rise out of the water and appear to float at the horizon.

(616) 426-4013

MOST-POPULAR DUNE CLIMBS

SLEEPING BEAR DUNE.
Sleeping Bear Dunes National Lakeshore, Empire.

On sunny summer days, thousands of park visitors make the tough slog 150 feet up the feels-like-vertical east face of the world's most-famous sand dune. From the summit of the mountain of hot, soft sand, views east over Glen Lake are nice, but to get to Lake Michigan you've got to hike west another two miles (one-way) across the sandy, hilly plateau. Consequently, most sand-mountaineers make a rapid (running, rolling and tumbling for kids) descent to an ice cream stand at the bottom.

(231) 326-5134

TOWER HILL AND PIKES PEAK.
Warren Dunes State Park, Bridgman.

It often appears as though half of the 20,000 visitors who enter Michigan's most-visited park each summer weekend make at least one trip up these steep, adjoining sand mountains, which rise up only a few hundred yards behind an immense sandy beach. From the peaks, excellent views over Lake Michigan sometimes include Chicago's skyline (see entry, top left).

(616) 426-4013

RAREST ORV PARK

SILVER LAKE STATE PARK. Mears.

The Midwest's only designated off-road-vehicle area in sand dunes is a 450-acre parcel at the north end of this popular state park. Dune buggies, dirt bikes, trucks, trail jeeps and other types of ORVs, some of which are rented from a nearby concessionaire, roar over the busy area from April 1 through October 1.

(231) 873-3083

RAREST DUNE RIDES

MAC WOOD'S DUNE RIDES. Mears. (231) 873-2817
SAUGATUCK DUNE RIDES. Saugatuck. (231) 857-2253

The state's only privately owned dune-ride concessions are near-identical combinations of thrill ride/educational tour over some of the massive mounds of sugar-fine sand that line our west coast. Dune schooners — "stretch" fat-tired 4WD pickups missing their tops and doors — carry up to 15 passengers at a time on 45-minute serpentine, roller-coaster trips over acres of white sand, with brief pauses for scenic looks at Lake Michigan, inland lakes tucked into the dunes, and unique natural features such as sand-blast-sculpted dunewood and chunks of glass created by lightning strikes.

QUICKEST, COMPREHENSIVE DUNE PRIMER

GILLETTE NATURE CENTER.
Hoffmaster State Park, Muskegon.

The nearly three miles of Lake Michigan shoreline that edges P.J. Hoffmaster State Park is part of the world's longest fresh-water stretch of sand dunes. Centering the park is the Gillette Nature Center, where hands-on displays, multi-image slide shows, dioramas and other professionally prepared exhibits provide a superior, substantive introduction to the natural history of dunes and fragile dune ecology. Most visitors further their education by hiking adjoining interpretive trails and climbing nearly 200 stairs to an outstanding dune-top view (p. 30).

(231) 798-3573

MOST-EXPANSIVE NO-FRILLS DUNE EXPERIENCE

NORDHOUSE DUNES WILDERNESS AREA. Manistee.

This 4,300-acre tract is the state's only large, undeveloped parcel of public dune land. Motorized vehicles are prohibited, and so the only way to explore the rugged, scenic natural area is on foot, either on or off 10 miles of designated trails that wind past backcountry campsites and a long, sandy swimming beach.

(231) 723-2211

MOST-PICTURE-PERFECT DUNE PERSPECTIVE

SAND DUNES OF THE GREAT LAKES
(Sleeping Bear Press) by C.J. & Edna Effront

More than 140 exceptional full-color photos in this hardbound volume capture the full and varied beauty, character and appeal of the vast collection of sand dunes spread around Michigan's coastline.

MOST-SURREALISTIC DUNE SCENE

SILVER LAKE STATE PARK. Mears.
The view from a small beach/picnic area on the east shore of Silver Lake "is like no other in the state," says Tom Powers in *Michigan State and National Parks: A Complete Guide* (Friede Publications). "Looking completely out of place, a wall of sand rises out of, towers (100-200 feet) over, and *is* the lake's (1½-mile-long) west shore."
(231) 873-3083

MOST-EXPANSIVE WADING POOL

SCOTT'S POINT. Gould City.
At some spots along this beautiful, easy-to-get-to but secluded, sandy beach that stretches for miles along Lake Michigan, the water is only ankle-deep even hundreds of feet out from shore. An added plus: the view of the Beaver Island Archipelago, 10 miles to the south, is the closest across Lake Michigan from anywhere in the state.

MOST-ACCESSIBLE, LITTLE-USED, SANDY GREAT LAKES BEACH

PT. AU CHENES TO U.S.F.S LAKE MICHIGAN CAMP AND PICNIC GROUNDS.
US-2 travelers can pull off onto the wide shoulder just about anywhere along this 4-mile stretch of beautiful, sandy, wide Lake Michigan beach bisected by the Breevort River. Despite the easy access, few motorists stretch their legs here, most likely because there are no facilities.

MOST-EXPANSIVE STATE-PARK BEACH TO COMB

WILDERNESS STATE PARK. Carp Lake.
"You can wander nearly deserted (Lake Michigan) beaches for days without crossing the same sand twice," says Tom Powers about this out-of-the-way state park. The author of *Michigan State and National Parks: A Complete Guide* (Friede Publications) also says that trails from the park's 30 miles of finger-shaped coastline — ranging from white sand to rocky limestone — lead into one of the Lower Peninsula's largest tracts of wilderness.
(231) 436-5381

CHOICEST GUIDE TO ON-THE-BEATEN PATHS

TRAIL ATLAS OF MICHIGAN
(Hansen Publishing) by Dennis Hansen

Hikers, mountain bikers, cross-country skiers, and other nonmotorized outdoor lovers in search of new routes should amble through this thorough 659-page trail-reference guide. The regularly updated compendium provides one or more maps and essential details — including distances, directions to trailhead, terrain, ski-grooming methods, and ratings and difficulty levels for each type of activity — for each of more than 600 trails throughout the state.

GREATEST INSIDE OUTDOOR SHOW

OUTDOORAMA. Novi Expo Center.
The state's oldest and largest all-around, great-outdoors sport and travel show features 450 exhibits, including recreational vehicles, fishing and power boats, small-scale custom log homes, live wildlife, and the latest hunting, fishing, and camping equipment and accessories. The 10-day event, sponsored each February by the Michigan United Conservation Club, is also an excellent place to book guided adventures offered by a huge selection of fly-in services and camps, outfitters, full-service lodges, booking agents, resorts and campgrounds from all over North America.
(800) 777-6720   www.mucc.org

BEST SOMETHING-FOR-EVERYONE STATE PARKS

LUDINGTON STATE PARK. Ludington.

Hunts' Highlights of Michigan (Midwestern Guides) calls Ludington, "the best all-rounded of Michigan's many state parks;" Tom Powers in *Michigan State and National Parks: A Complete Guide* (Friede Publications) describes it as "one of Michigan's finest outdoor playgrounds;" and recently, *Detroit News* readers rated the park #1 in the state-run system.

And all for good reason. More than 5,000 acres between Lake Michigan and Hamlin Lake take in the connecting Sable River; six miles of beautiful, sandy Lake Michigan beach; scenic dunes; an historic lighthouse, an interpretive center; and 18 miles of trails. Together they offer an outstanding mix of camping, picnicking, hiking, biking, jogging, cross country skiing, hunting, fishing, boating, swimming, canoeing, tubing and other recreational opportunities.

(231) 843-2423

PORCUPINE MOUNTAINS STATE PARK. Ontonagon.

For people who like to actively immerse themselves in the out-of-doors, Michigan's largest state park has it all, including

- 90 miles of rugged hiking trails that criss-cross rushing rivers, skirt pristine lakes, pass by more than 30 scenic waterfalls and climb to spectacular vistas
- backcountry camping in Adirondack-type shelters or rustic one-room cabins scattered throughout 60,000 acres of forested hills
- bear, deer and bird hunting opportunities
- fishing, from tossing flies at backcountry brook trout to trolling the big waters of Lake Superior

And in the winter, says *Detroit News* outdoor columnist Eric Sharp, the Porkies serve up "the finest cross-country skiing in North America; an excellent downhill ski area (p. 34)..., snowshoe trails that look like Alaska, and snowmobiling that usually lasts into April."

(906) 885-5275

MOST-COMPREHENSIVE STATE PARK GUIDE

MICHIGAN STATE AND NATIONAL PARKS: A COMPLETE GUIDE
(Friede Publications) by Tom Powers

The author not only describes but also honestly evaluates camping, hiking, skiing, hunting, fishing and other recreational opportunities available at each of Michigan's 96 state parks. A large map and photo for each helps show what to expect, and the book is updated regularly.

An added bonus is similar treatment of four national parks and lakeshores in the state.

BEST STATE PARK TO REALLY, *REALLY* GET AWAY FROM IT ALL

CRAIG LAKE STATE PARK. Champion.

Hikers, backpackers, canoers, kayakers, fishermen and hunters who like their outdoor experiences truly wild, nonmotorized and solitary can figuratively — and if not careful, literally — lose themselves in this large, out-of-the-way, primitive park. Only a two-track access road and a few designated trails mark the park's 7,000 beautiful wilderness acres, which include seven lakes. Wheeled vehicles and boat motors are banned, and the few bushwackers and paddlers who come to Michigan's least-visited state park rarely encounter other people, only wildlife, including moose and wolves.

(906) 339-4461

MOST-POPULAR STATE PARK

WARREN DUNES. Bridgman.

Each year nearly a million and a half visitors — many from Chicago and other out-of-state areas — immerse themselves in this park's 1,523 acres of Lake Michigan sand piled into huge dunes and spread over one of the state's largest, most-beautiful beaches.

(616) 426-4013

BEST STATE-RUN SKI RUNS

PORCUPINE MOUNTAINS STATE PARK. Ontonagon.

The largest ski complex in any Michigan state park includes a triple chairlift, a double chairlift, a T-bar and a handle-tow that transport downhill skiers to 14 runs, totaling 11 miles down 640 vertical feet, the biggest drop of any ski area in the state. An added plus: the area is also one of the most-affordable — especially for families — in the state.

(906) 885-5275

QUICKEST DOWNHILL RIDE UP

CRYSTAL MOUNTAIN. Thompsonville.

Billed as the fastest chairlift in the Midwest, the Crystal Clipper can transport 40 skiers per minute from the front of this resort's lodge up 500 feet to the start of 13 different downhill runs.

(800) 968-4676   www.crystalmtn.com

LONGEST DOWNHILL SKI RUN

WEASEL GULCH. Marquette Mountain, Marquette.

This fun beginner tuck-run cuts a narrow, 8,300-foot-long swath through woods home to feeding deer as it gently winds and drops 600 feet down the side of Marquette Mountain.

(800) 944-7669   www.marquettemountain.com

STEEPEST SKI RUN

COULOIR. Boyne Highlands, Harbor Springs.

With a 90-percent grade, this sphincter-tightening (or possibly -loosening), narrow, hour-glass-shaped run is the steepest in the Midwest.

(800) 462-6963   www.boyne.com

MOST DOWNHILL SKI RUNS

BOYNE MOUNTAIN. Boyne Falls.

49

(800) 462-6963   www.boyne.com

BEST FAMILY SKI RESORT

CRYSTAL MOUNTAIN. Thompsonville.

Creative, first-rate on- and off-slope facilities, activities and amenities geared to age and ability are reasons this resort consistently ranks as one of the *country's* best for families.

Supervised day care for infants and toddlers is available in a home-like environment that includes a kitchen and a nap area with cribs and cozy beds. Willing three- and four-year-olds can get indoor pre-ski instruction plus some protected outdoor experience. Eager five and six-year-olds can hit the slopes, where team-taught ski games and activities help them gain confidence while learning the basics. Fun ski classes for 7-12 year olds are grouped by age and ability levels, and many preteens and teens gravitate to snowboarding lessons.

Skiers of all ages and abilities drop down a choice of 34 slopes, ranging from gentle, meandering beginner to challenging expert runs, more than a dozen of which are lighted for night skiing.

And apres-ski options include a swimming pool, a hot tub, fitness center, ice skating, snowshoeing, and sleigh rides.

(800) 968-4676   www.crystalmtn.com

BEST MICHIGAN WEBSITES FOR MICHIGAN DOWNHILL SKIERS

WWW.MICHIGANSKIER.COM
WWW.MICHIWEB.COM/SKI

Using these two similar sites, downhill skiers can get just about all information needed for successful spur-of-the-moment or thoroughly planned Michigan excursions. Of immediate value in season are current conditions — base, new-snow, surface, and weather — plus maps and other pertinent info for each of the state's 42 major downhill areas. Mouse clicks also call up events calendars, directories, lists of schools and associations, plus links to articles and columns and individual resort websites.

BEST GOLF WEB LINK

WWW.MLIVE.COM/GOLF

Michigan has more public-access golf courses (more than 700 and growing) than any other state and ranks third in total number of courses (nearly a thousand and growing). Golfers can sort through the plethora of diverse public options by keystroking to this fast-loading, up-to-date website, which features course reviews, virtual lessons, golf news, and articles about the sport's personalities, rules and equipment. And mouse clicks through an easy-to-use directory also call up slope, yardage, par, pricing and other useful information for nearly every public course in the state.

MOST-INTENSE FORE-PLAY

Jackson claims to have more golf holes per capita than any American city except Sarasota, Florida. "Golf is an obsession in Jackson," says *Hunts' Highlights of Michigan* (Midwestern Guides), and "the high quality of its public and municipal courses makes it available to virtually everybody."

Oakland has more golf courses — 93, including 64 that are open to the public — than any other Michigan county.

With 22 top-flight courses — many the signatures of prestigious designers — greater Gaylord has earned a reputation as the Midwest's "Golf Mecca." Golfers who make the pilgrimage can even book tee times while checking in at area motels.

MOST-SPECTACULAR GOLF COURSE

BAY HARBOR GOLF CLUB.

All the experts rank Bay Harbor's 27 diverse, often-dramatic holes and unmatched setting as one of the country's — some say the world's — top golf experiences. A trio of nine-hole courses are spread atop 170-foot bluffs, through acres of sand dunes, and to the edges of giant rock escarpments along more than five miles of breathtaking Lake Michigan shoreline, leading many to label the resort the "Pebble Beach of the Midwest."

(800) 462-6963   www.boyne.com

BEST ISLAND GOLF GETAWAYS

THE ROCK, DRUMMOND ISLAND

Created by blasting away tons of limestone and hauling in tons of dirt, the secluded, 400-acre scenic setting of this 18-hole Woodmoor Resort course now includes wildflowers, ponds, lakes, waterfalls, wildlife (including bears) and unique rock outcroppings.

(800) 999-6343   www.drummondisland.com

THE JEWEL, MACKINAC ISLAND

While playing this 18-hole Grand Hotel course, golfers are treated to spectacular views of the Straits of Mackinac, Mackinac Island's well-known commercial district, and the hotel itself. And unique to any Michigan course, at the turn, golfers are transported to the 10th tee by horse-drawn carriage.

(906) 847-3331   www.grandhotel.com

WAWASHKAMO GOLF CLUB, MACKINAC ISLAND

This relatively unknown, one-of-a-kind golf destination has been rated by *Golf Magazine* as one of the top-10 nine-hole courses in the world. It is also the first nine-hole course designated as an Historic Golf Landmark by *Golf Digest* and for good reasons. The course is a century old, horse-drawn mowers cut the grass, the watering system is mostly rain, golfers can tee off from sand, the rough is really rough, and tiny greens require careful approaches.

(906) 847-3871   www.wawashkamo.com

HIGHEST-RATED SCOTTISH-STYLE LINKS

THE GAILES, LAKEWOOD SHORES. Oscoda.

At this Lake Huron resort, golfers have the rare opportunity to experience the design, strategy and character of the game as played in its birthplace. Rated by *Golf Digest* in 1993 as the country's best new resort course and three years later as *the* best course in Michigan, all 18 Gailes holes faithfully replicate the unique features of top Scottish courses, including double greens (which serve two holes), heather, hidden pot bunkers and small creeks, and undulating bent-grass fairways (also some doubles) that flow into greens mowed only slightly lower.

(800) 882-2493   www.lakewoodshores.com

BEST WALKING-ONLY COURSE

THE TRADITION. Gaylord.

This classic 18-hole, par-70 course at Sylvan Treetops Resort was designed by renowned golf instructor Rick Smith specifically for golfers who love to chase their shots on foot. Walker-friendly details include gently rolling, partially wooded terrain; short yardage (4,907 to 6,467, depending on tees used); wide fairways; moderate bunkering; and greens and tees situated close to each other. Walking, in fact, is mandatory here; carts are banned. But for those who don't want to carry their own bag, caddies are available.

(888) 873-3867   www.treetops.com

MOST-POPULAR BRIDGE WALK

MACKINAC BRIDGE WALK.
Mackinaw City/St. Ignace.

This annual Labor Day celebration is the only time pedestrians are allowed on the state's best-known landmark. Each year 40,000-60,000 walkers take advantage of the rare opportunity to enjoy a unique perspective of the imposing structure and surrounding scenery while making the 5-mile crossing.

(800) 666-0160   www.mackinawcity.com
(800) 338-6660   www.stignace.com

BEST MICHIGAN WEBSITE FOR MICHIGAN RUNNERS

WWW.MICHIGANRUNNER.COM

Michigan Runner magazine, considered the bible of state foot racers, hosts this site, which features up-to-date local and national running news, resources, training tips, race results, access to past issues of the magazine, links to other regional publications, and a border-to-border listing and schedule of upcoming Michigan races.

MOST-POPULAR 10K RUN

TURKEY TROT. Detroit.

This annual Thanksgiving Day run through downtown Detroit draws more than 5,000 entrants (all but about 500 who finish), making it the largest 10K run in the state and one of the largest in the nation.

(248) 544-9099   www.motorcitystriders.com

TOP-RANKED 10-MILE RUN

THE CRIM 10-MILE. Flint.

This internationally renowned 10-mile event is the only one in the state to make respected *Runner's World* magazine's list of the nation's top-100 road races based on "participation, organization, reputation, community involvement, spirit, uniqueness, location and competition." In addition to attracting the world's best 10-milers after $53,000 in prize money, the late-August, two-day festival also draws 15,000 amateurs to 1-mile, 5K and 8K runs and walks plus a series of noncompetitive children's Teddy Bear Trots.

(810) 235-3396   www.crim.org

MOST-POPULAR 25K RUN

THE OLD KENT RIVER BANK RUN.
Grand Rapids.

With some 4,000 entrants, this annual May event consistently ranks at or near the top of the country's largest 25K runs, according to *On the Road Magazine*, the official newsletter of USA Track and Field.

(616) 771-1590   www.okriverbankrun.com

MOST-RELAXING HIGH-STAKES TRIATHLON

CORPORATE CHALLENGE. Garland Resort, Lewiston.

Each October, four-member teams pay $10,000 per squad to compete in a unique three-day golfing/hunting/fishing triathlon. The team that accumulates the most points after one day each of 18-hole golf, European-style pheasant hunting, and fly and spincasting for trout, pike and bluegill gets their entry fee refunded.

(800) 968-0042   www.garlandusa.com

BEST BICYCLE-TOURING COMPANY

MICHIGAN BICYCLE TOURING. Kingsley.

Variety, consistent attention to detail, and lots of fun are reasons individuals and families have filled Michigan Bicycle Touring's day, weekend and five-day guided bike excursions since 1977. The Keweenaw Wayfarer, Saugatuck Amble, Woodland Odyssey and a dozen and a half other recreational tours combine scenic, small-group pedaling with a menu of other activities such as shopping, hiking, camping, kayaking and canoeing. Everything's-taken-care-of options also include routes geared to ability and a variety of interesting places to stay, such as the Big Bay Point Lighthouse (p. 26).

(231) 263-5885   www.bikembt.com

MOST-POPULAR ONE-DAY BIKE RIDE

APPLE CIDER CENTURY. Three Oaks.

The Midwest's largest one-day recreational bike tour, held annually the last Saturday in September, is so popular that entry is limited to 7,000 cyclists. Participants choose from 25-, 50-, 75- or 100-mile well-marked routes that skirt the shore of Lake Michigan and wind on scenic country roads past orchards and vineyards. And before, during and after the noncompetitive event, they are treated to a spaghetti dinner, an ice cream social and, of course, several thousand gallons of apple cider.

(616) 756-3361   http://welcome.to/applecidercentury

MOST-SPECTACULAR ISLAND BIKE CIRCUIT

GRAND ISLAND. Munising.

Pictured Rocks, the Grand Sable Dunes, sheer sandstone bluffs, a picturesque lighthouse and sandy Lake Superior beaches are included in the many spectacular, often high-level views that come from a 22-mile biking/hiking lakeshore trail around this newly created, nearly undeveloped 13,000-acre national recreation area. Cyclists reach the gravel route, which is rated moderate to difficult, via ferry from Munising, where regular but not mountain rental bikes are available.

(906) 387-3503   www.mmba.org

MOST-POPULAR ISLAND BIKE RIDE

M-185, MACKINAC ISLAND.

I've never seen statistics to prove it, but I'd bet that nearly flat, scenic, cars-banned, 8-mile-long highway M-185, which circles Mackinac Island, is the most-traveled bike route in the state.

BEST MICHIGAN MOUNTAIN-BIKING GUIDEBOOKS

"No other state in the Midwest has the mileage or the variety (of mountain biking trails) that (Michigan) does," an official of the International Mountain Bicycling Association has claimed. And no books are better at detailing the state's best on- and off-road opportunities than the *Mountain Biking Michigan* series (Thunder Bay Press), which includes

The Best Trails in the Upper Peninsula
    by Mike McLelland and Karen Gentry

The Best Trails in Northern Lower Michigan
    by Mike Terrell

The Best Trails in Southern Michigan
    by Dwain Abramowski and Sandra Davison

The three volumes cover more than 120 routes ranging from flat, scenic rides to tortuous, technical trails. The authors personally pedaled every mile, and so their maps and detailed descriptions are accurate and authoritative.

MOST-TECHNICALLY DIFFICULT MOUNTAIN-BIKE TRAIL

HIGHLAND RECREATION AREA. Oakland County.

Almost all knowledgeable Michigan mountain bikers agree that the 14.5-mile root-marred, log-strewn, tree-canopied bike trail that twists through the hilly Highland Recreation Area requires more off-road skills than any other route in the state. Included is a section consistently ranked as the "hardest four miles of mountain biking in Michigan."

(248) 889-3750   www.mmba.org

EASIEST INTERNATIONAL BIKE BORDER CROSSING

INTERNATIONAL BRIDGE. Sault Ste. Marie.

Bicyclists can ride across this 3-mile-long bridge to and from Canada after paying a 75-cent toll. Bicyclists are prohibited from crossing the Ambassador Bridge (Detroit) and are taken across the Blue Water Bridge (Port Huron) in official transport vehicles only at the convenience of bridge personnel.

(906) 635-5255

COOLEST CANADIAN CROSSOVER

DRUMMOND ISLAND.

For about 10 weeks each winter, several thousand snowmobilers and a few mountain bikers make trips across the only official ice bridge between the United States and Canada. Two routes begin at Potagannissing Bay, with one running 12 miles northwest to St. Joseph Island, Ontario, and the other 20 miles to Thessalon, Ontario. Each trail across the frozen St. Mary's River is marked with rows of used Christmas trees and is staffed with a customs officer at each end.

(800) 737-8666

MOST-BEAUTIFUL, ACCESSIBLE FROZEN CAVES

ROCK RIVER WILDERNESS AREA. Chatham.

In winter, water that seeps from and drips over the top of limestone walls that line the Rock River Valley, creates numerous sparkling "ice caves." Area snowshoers and cross country skiers take advantage of the unique opportunity to crawl between the rock walls and thick, 15-foot-long icicles suspended from overhangs.

(906) 225-8687

BEST PLACE TO CLIMB THE WALLS

PLANET ROCK. Pontiac.

The state's largest climbing gym features 13,500 square feet of climbing area that includes 55-foot walls, one motorized wall, and a bouldering cave with hand holds on the walls and roof. The facility also rents necessary equipment and offers an inexpensive one-day introduction to the thrill sport of rock climbing. And unique to Michigan's indoor climbs, children as young as five are allowed to participate.

(248) 334-3904

BEST PLACE TO SCALE ICE

MUNISING.

From December through April, water that spills, seeps and flows over Munising/Grand Island-area cliffs freezes, thaws, refreezes and continually flows to create what is promoted as the best climbing ice in the Midwest. Individuals, guided groups, and climbing-club members from around the country agree. They regularly haul in crampons, ice axes, harnesses, helmets, ropes, ice screws and carabiners and create routes up the frozen waterfalls, 100-yard-wide ice curtains, 30-foot-in-diameter columns, "chimneys," leaning walls, and other challenging formations.

(906) 226-7112

BEST LOWER-PENINSULA CLIMBING CLIFF

OAK PARK. Grand Ledge.

The Lower Peninsula's only natural, accessible rock formation worth climbing is a 600-foot-long section in a mile of soft sandstone outcroppings along the Grand River west of Lansing. Climbers of all abilities make their way up the steep, 40-foot-high cliff using nature-created toeholds and finger slots along any of approximately 50 established routes with names such as The Nose, Potato Chips, Despondency, and Intimidation.

MOST-FLAMBOYANT ROUTE TO THE TOP

Detroit Free Press

On July 4, 1983, two urban mountaineers, using special gripping devices, made an unauthorized 6½-hour climb up the outside of Michigan's highest manmade peak, the 74-story Marriott (formerly Westin) Hotel at Detroit's Renaissance Center. The "human flies," were arrested for trespassing and disorderly conduct, but the charges were dismissed because the hotel had not posted any "no trespassing" signs on the outside of the building.

MOST-POPULAR U.P. CLIMBING CLIFFS

PALMER CLIFFS. Palmer.

A short drive from this small village southwest of Marquette, followed by a short hike ends at the edge of 90-foot-high, solid quartzite cliffs used as a teaching area for the Northern Michigan University climbing classes.

BOLDEST PRISON ESCAPES

SOUTHERN MICHIGAN PRISON, JACKSON. June 6, 1975.

The friend of a convicted hog thief and rubber-check artist chartered a helicopter, then forced the pilot at knife point to swoop over the prison walls and land out of guards' firing range at a spot marked by a red handkerchief. The inmate, who had been hiding between two buildings, darted aboard and made his escape only to be captured 30 hours later.

MARQUETTE STATE PRISON. September 25, 1939.

Four prisoners armed with knives overpowered a guard, burst into an afternoon meeting of the Parole Board, and took the chairman, a board member and the prison's warden and deputy warden as hostages. The convicts then commandeered a prison car and led a 14-car posse of sheriff's deputies, city police, and state police on a wild 90-mph, 128-mile, three-hour chase before overturning and being captured. All hostages escaped or were released unharmed.

WATERSCAPES

NATURALLY BIGGEST BATHTUB

RAINY LAKE. Millersburg.

This unique 200-acre lake has holes and cracks in its bottom, usually sealed with sediment and debris, that connect to underground limestone chambers. After just the right, rare set of natural disturbances — as happened in 1894, 1925 and 1950 — the drains unplug and all of the water runs out. When mud and silt reseal the openings, the lake fills back up.

MOST-MOVING ISLAND

A one-acre island, complete with brush and 40-foot trees, floats around Lake Dubonnet, near Interlochen, at the whim of the wind. In 1956 controlled flooding from a dam created the 200-acre lake from two smaller ponds, and in the process large areas of lowland broke loose. For unknown reasons, one did not dissolve and has survived for more than 40 years as the floating island.

MOST-EXPANSIVE DELTA

ST. CLAIR FLATS. Harsens Island.

Tons of sediment carried over the centuries from the upper Great Lakes by the St. Clair River and dropped at the entrance to Lake St. Clair has created the largest delta in the Great Lakes. The scenic, roughly 30-square-mile area (including half in Canada) takes in dozens of islands, levees, dikes, marshes, and strips of land that appear to be floating on the water.

BEST WAY TO LOCATE WATERFALLS

A GUIDE TO 199 MICHIGAN WATERFALLS (Friede Publications) by the Penrose family

This outstanding practical guide not only describes and often shows black-and-white photos of Michigan's many beautiful waterfalls but also pinpoints their locations with detailed maps and directions.

PRETTIEST ROADSIDE WATERFALLS

According to *A Guide to 199 Michigan Waterfalls* (Friede Publications), you can view the following scenic waterfalls without leaving your vehicle, plus get closer looks by making easy walks from roadside parking areas.

ALGER FALLS
M-28, one mile south of Munising.

EAGLE RIVER FALLS
M-26, Eagle River.

FUMEE FALLS
Lien Roadside Park, US-2 3½ miles northwest of Norway

HAVEN FALLS
Haven Park, Lac La Belle.

JACOBS FALLS
M-26, 3 miles north of Eagle River.

RAPID RIVER FALLS
S-15, ¼ mile west of US-41,
6½ miles north of Rapid River.

REANY FALLS
Forestville Road, 3 miles northwest of Marquette.

SCOTT FALLS
Rathfoot Park, M-28 2 miles east of AuTrain.

WARNER FALLS
M-35, ½ mile south of Palmer.

UPPER FALLS, FALLS RIVER

MANABEZHO FALLS

GORGE FALLS

MOST-SPECTACULAR WATERFALL CLUSTERS

BLACK RIVER. Bessemer.

From parking areas along a 3-mile stretch of County Road 513, short trails lead through hardwood and hemlock forests to splendid views of five distinctly beautiful waterfalls — Great Conglomerate, Gorge, Potawatomi, Sandstone and Rainbow.

FALLS RIVER. L'Anse.

"If we had to recommend just one river to visit in all of Michigan, this would be it," say the Penrose family in *A Guide to 199 Michigan Waterfalls* (Friede Publications). The fast-flowing river drops over a minimum of eight beautiful, easily reached falls as it rushes its final 3½ miles through the town of L'Anse and into Lake Superior.

PRESQUE ISLE RIVER. Porcupine Mountains State Park.

As this powerful river forces its way through a gorge on its final mile to Lake Superior, it divides its 125-foot plummet among four gorgeous falls — Nawadaha, Manido, Manabezho and one unnamed. Excellent views of all come from either a streamside path or at the end of short trails from parking areas along County Road 519.

(906) 885-5275

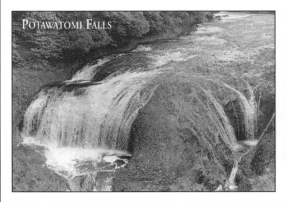

POTAWATOMI FALLS

BIGGEST, BEST-KNOWN WATERFALL

UPPER TAHQUAMENON FALLS. Paradise.

As the main attraction at its namesake state park, Michigan's largest waterfall (and the third-largest east of the Mississippi) is also the state's most familiar, most visited, and most photographed. All for good reason; it's spectacular. Each second during normal conditions, 50,000 gallons of the hemlock-stained Tahquamenon River roar over a 200-foot-wide ledge and drop 50 feet in a gold-, amber- and white-striped water wall.

(906) 492-3415

BIGGEST INDOOR WATER DROP

A 114-foot-tall, 20-foot-wide marble fountain shaped like a grouping of several dozen skyscrapers was listed by the *Guinness Book of World Records* (Guinness Media, Inc.) as the world's tallest indoor waterfall. The sculpture helps form one wall of Detroit Greektown's International Center building.

MOST-ELABORATE MAN-MADE WATERFALL

CASCADES. Jackson.

Each summer evening in Cascade Park, 3,000 gallons of water a minute drops 500 feet through a 30-foot-wide concrete flume divided into steps to create 16 minifalls. Six spraying fountains pump the water while recorded music plays, and after dark more than a thousand lights create changing patterns of color.

(517) 788-4320

MOST-BEAUTIFUL SPRING

KITCH-ITI-KIPI. Palms Book State Park, Manistique.

Michigan's largest spring is also one of the state's most-uniquely beautiful natural attractions. The incredible clarity of its cold water allows views down 40 feet to a white/gray sand bottom painted by multicolored mosses and algae and interrupted by 20 roiling inlets.

(906) 341-2355

MOST STREAMLINED SMALL SWAMP

TIMBERLAND SWAMP. Clarkston.

This 800-acre wetlands, surrounded by a 245-acre nature preserve at the fringes of metro Detroit, is the humble origin of three major rivers — the Huron, Shiawassee and a branch of the Clinton.

BIGGEST DRAIN

SAGINAW RIVER. Saginaw.

As the single spigot for water flowing from a total of 22 different counties covering one-sixth of the Lower Peninsula, the confluence of the Flint, Shiawassee, Tittabawassee, and Cass rivers to form the 20-mile-long Saginaw River (Michigan's shortest) is the largest watershed in the state.

MOST-VISITED UNSEEN STREAM

Few of the 100,000-plus fans who pack each University of Michigan home football game are aware that Allen's Creek — a sometimes-drainage ditch, mostly underground spring — flows underneath their team's playing field. When the stands are empty, report groundskeepers and security personnel, you can put your ear down on the 50 yard line and hear the flowing water.

BEST BOOK TO HAVE WHEN UP A CREEK *WITH* A PADDLE

CANOEING MICHIGAN RIVERS (Friede Publications) by Jerry Dennis and Craig Date

The authors personally canoed more than 1,500 miles on 45 select Michigan rivers in order to authoritatively detail opportunities available to paddlers of all abilities. An easy-to-follow map for each river includes access sites, rapids, roads, bridges and other essentials.

BEST URBAN CANOEING RIVER

HURON RIVER. Milford to Lake Erie.

For a river that flows through some of the state's most-heavily populated areas — including Ann Arbor, Ypsilanti, and southern metro Detroit — the Huron is clean and, outside the urban areas, relatively wild and undeveloped. Added pluses for recreational canoeists are the many access points, few hazards, slow to moderate current, and large number of outstanding parks and recreation areas connected by the 100 or so miles of canoeable water.

BEST FAMILY PADDLES

Jerry Dennis, author of *Canoeing Michigan Rivers* (Friede Publications) and the foremost authority on where to paddle in Michigan, rates the following rivers as the state's best for family canoeing. All offer a uniquely appealing mix of accessibility, usually gentle current, and scenery, including significant sections through undeveloped areas with opportunities to observe wildlife. Several liveries with rentals are spread along the lengths of the Lower Peninsula rivers, sections of which are also suitable for tubing.

SOUTHERN MICHIGAN
> **Huron River**, especially from Kent Lake Dam to Baseline Lake Dam and from Hudson Mills Metropark to Ann Arbor.

WESTERN MICHIGAN
> **Flat River**, with the sections from Greenville Dam to Belding Dam and Belding Dam to Fallasburg Park particularly appealing.

NORTHEAST MICHIGAN
> **Au Sable River**, main stream and South Branch, with the most-popular trips on the main stream running from Grayling to Wakeley Bridge and from Mio Dam to McKinley Bridge.

NORTHWEST MICHIGAN
> **Manistee River**

WESTERN UPPER PENINSULA
> **Michigamme River**

EAST-CENTRAL UPPER PENINSULA
> **Manistique River**, with Dennis particularly recommending the section through the Seney National Wildlife Refuge and from there to Merwin Creek Campground.

MOST-POPULAR FLOAT

MUSKEGON RIVER AT BIG RAPIDS.

Each summer more than 35,000 tubers, often a thousand in a single day, make a leisurely two-hour float from the Sawmill Canoe Livery through downtown Big Rapids to Highbanks Park, making that slow-moving segment of the Muskegon River the most-tubed waterway in the state, according to the livery's owners.

(231) 796-6408

MOST-CHALLENGING WHITEWATER RIVER

Craig Date

PRESQUE ISLE RIVER. Porcupine Mountains State Park.

Experienced canoeists and kayakers rank the last 17½ miles of the Presque Isle, just before it empties into Lake Superior, as the most difficult, unpredictable, hazardous stretch of river in Michigan, some say the Midwest. Difficult rapids and falls, constricted passages, rapid descent and turbulent waters through a wild, near-inaccessible area are among reasons *Canoe* magazine once listed the Presque Isle as one of only 10 North American rivers that "define the outer edge of contemporary whitewater paddling."

(906) 885-5275

WILDEST WHITEWATER RAFTING

MENOMINEE RIVER.

Whitewater rafting enthusiasts from throughout the Midwest converge on the Piers Gorge section of this river, which forms the border between the western Upper Peninsula and Wisconsin. Experienced rafters paddling their own craft and novices on three-hour guided group expeditions all take on "one of Michigan's fiercest stretches of river," says Jerry Dennis in *Canoeing Michigan Rivers* (Friede Publications), with plenty of "drops and chutes with back-rollers, souse holes and other hazards (with names like Hell Hole and Volkswagen Rock)."

(715) 251-3886
(715) 757-3431   w.kosirs.com

PRETTIEST PLACE
TO TAKE SEA-KAYAKING LESSONS

MUNISING.

Expert paddlers from Northern Waters Sea Kayaking give wanna-be sea kayakers an hour's group instruction on Lake Superior next to the imposing, monolithic Pictured Rocks National Lakeshore rock formation named Miners Castle (p. 30). The novices are then guided east for intimate, quiet looks at the rest of the lakeshore's beautiful, naturally sculpted, colorful cliffs. Weather permitting, side trips include probes into sea caves and a paddle *through* Lower Chapel Falls. When north winds are blowing, the floating classroom shifts to the sheltered, also-picturesque coves of Grand Island.

(906) 387-2323 and off-season (715) 356-9092

SUPERIOR SEA-KAYAKING ROUTE

KEWEENAW WATER TRAIL.

This 47-mile designated recreational water pathway across the Keweenaw Peninsula is Michigan's only operational section of the Lake Superior Water Trail, a scenic water route with regularly accessible facilities that if completed will circuit the world's second-largest freshwater lake. Best experienced by sea kayak, the beautiful Keweenaw segment follows the Portage Waterway from Keweenaw Bay through Portage Lake past Houghton/Hancock to McClain State Park.

SMOOTHEST TALL-SHIP SAILING

MANITOU. Northport.

One of the Great Lakes largest sailing vessels carries up to 24 passengers on multiday "windjammer" cruises. Itinerary is at the whim of wind and weather, but usual destinations for the 114-foot-long, two-masted topsail schooner include northern Lake Michigan coastal villages, Sleeping Bear Dunes National Lakeshore, and Manitou, Beaver, Mackinac, Drummond and North Channel islands.

(231) 941-2000   www.tallshipsailing.com

MOST-CREATIVE CROSSING

In August 1969 a 32-year-old East Lansing man made a 65-mile, 14½-hour voyage across Lake Michigan in a bathtub welded to a frame supported by four 30-gallon oil drums and propelled by a 20-horsepower outboard motor.

MOST-SPECTACULAR INLAND WATER ROUTES

Michigan's two most-beautiful, diverse, lengthy inland waterway systems offer a unique blend of outstanding scenery, wildlife, picturesque villages, parks, beaches, restaurants, motels and shopping. Boaters can launch their own craft at several ramps or rent, preferably a pontoon boat, from resorts and marinas along the routes.

CHAIN OF LAKES. Antrim County.

Beginning at Six Mile Lake near Ellsworth, this spring-fed water network twists an uninterrupted 65 miles through a dozen and a half other lakes and rivers to Elk Rapids at Lake Michigan. Included in the chain are the Skegemog Lake Wildlife Area, 7,700-acre Elk Lake, and Torch Lake, Michigan's second-largest and one of the *world's* four most beautiful lakes, according to *National Geographic* magazine.

INLAND WATERWAY. Cheboygan and Emmet counties.

Three lakes — Burt (the state's third largest), Mullett (the state's fifth largest) and Crooked — plus the Cheboygan, Indian and Crooked rivers make up this spectacular 40-mile-long liquid highway that connects Cheboygan, at Lake Huron, to Conway, only 2½ air miles from Lake Michigan.

FERRY BEST SHORTCUT

IRONTON FERRY. Ironton.

One of the country's most-unique ferries is an engine-powered, cable-driven metal barge that annually transports more than 70,000 passenger vehicles, four at a time, 200 yards across the top of Lake Charlevoix's South Arm. For more than 70 years, the five-minute crossing has been a significant timesaver for locals and tourists driving between Charlevoix and Boyne City.

(231) 547-2101

RAREST ARMSTRONG-POWERED FERRY

SAUGATUCK CHAIN FERRY. Saugatuck.

The country's only hand-cranked chain ferry shuttles bicyclists and walkers 225 feet across the Kalamazoo River between downtown Saugatuck and Lake Michigan sand dunes and beaches.

(231) 857-5801 www.saugatuck.com

EASIEST WAY TO PICTURE THE PICTURED ROCKS

PICTURED ROCKS CRUISES. Munising.

The only way to take in all 15 miles of the spectacular, variegated, multishaped cliffs that give name to the Pictured Rocks is on a three-hour boat tour out of Munising. From nowhere on shore can you get a good look at the features that dominate the national lakeshore's west half—50- to 200-foot-high sandstone/limestone walls that glaciers, waves, frost and wind have carved into pillars, arches, caves and other unusual shapes, some with such distinct character that they have acquired names such as Miners Castle (p. 30), Chapel Rock, Battleship Row and Indian Head.

(906) 387-2379 and off season (906) 387-3820 www.picturedrocks.com

Pictured Rocks Cruises

Pictured Rocks Cruises

BEST ABOVE-WATER, UNDERWATER SHIPWRECK VIEWS

Shipwreck Tours, Inc. / Tom Buchkoe

GRAND ISLAND SHIPWRECK TOUR. Munising.

During a scenic, educational 2½-hour tour of the Grand Island area, the 60-foot glass-bottomed *Miss Munising* makes several slow passes over three major shipwrecks: 1) the scattered remains of the 210' wooden steamer *Herman Hettler*, which sank on its side during a 1926 storm; 2) the 130-year-old wreck of the *Burmuda*, a nearly intact 150-foot wood schooner whose deck is only 12 feet below the surface; and 3) the deckless skeleton of the 140' *Michael Groh*, a steambarge sunk in only nine feet of water.

Two large, covered viewing ports, clear water, and underwater boat lights for overcast days combine to guarantee outstanding views of the Lake Superior victims.

(906) 387-4477   www.shipwrecktours.com

SOUTH MANITOU ISLAND.

From a bluff on this island's south tip, you get a dramatic look down at the rusty hulk of the 246-foot Liberian freighter *Francisco Morazan*, which ran aground in 20 feet of water only 300 yards from shore during a November 1960 blizzard.

(231) 326-5134

BEST GUIDE TO LOOKING BELOW THE SURFACE

DIVERS GUIDE TO MICHIGAN
(Maritime Press) by Steve Harrington

This complete, detailed guide to skin and scuba diving emphasizes significant Great Lakes shipwrecks, particularly those in underwater preserves but also covers interesting dive sites in inland lakes and rivers and even around docks and wharves. Occasional pictures and drawings depict condition and orientation of wrecks, and appendixes list diving charters, downstate dive shops, recompression chambers and other resources.

MOST-COMPELLING SHIPWRECK MAUSOLEUM

GREAT LAKES SHIPWRECK MUSEUM.
Whitefish Point/Paradise.

Pieces of wrecks exhumed from a stretch of Lake Superior known as the "Graveyard of the Great Lakes" are displayed in this ghostly gallery. Funereal New Age music wafts through a large, dark viewing room where track lighting eerily illuminates remnants — the bell from the *Edmund Fitzgerald*, the broken helm of the *Superior City*, a gold wedding band retrieved from a skeleton — of a dozen fatal voyages.

(906) 635-1742   www.shipwreckmuseum.com

BEST MUSEUM SHIPS

S.S. KEEWATIN. Douglas.

Of the hundreds of coal-burning passenger steamships that cruised the Great Lakes during the early part of the 20th century, the *Keewatin* is the only one still afloat. Guided tours of the 350-foot vessel, permanently moored in the Kalamazoo River, reveal the dual — luxurious and spartan — nature of steamship travel. Passengers, for instance, ate gourmet meals in a mahogany-paneled dining room but slept in bunk beds in closet-size berths.

(616) 857-2107

VALLEY CAMP. Sault Ste. Marie.

This retired 550-foot-long, steam-powered Great Lakes freighter, permanently moored in the St. Mary's River, is a unique combination museum ship/maritime museum. Touring the floating behemoth's engine room, galley, mess hall, pilot house, captain's and crew's quarters, decks, hatches and other areas gives a vivid view of what life aboard all Great Lakes freighters is like.

And replacing cargo in the enormous holds is the world's largest Great Lakes maritime museum, which includes four 1,200-gallon aquariums, ship models, buoys, foghorns, anchors and two mangled lifeboats from Lake Superior's best-known victim, the *Edmund Fitzgerald.*

(906) 632-3658

HURON. Port Huron.

Until the 1960s, several Great Lakes shoals, reefs and other navigational hazards were marked by lightships, small vessels with bright beacons at the top of their masts. The only restored, preserved example of these unique "floating lighthouses," the 97-foot *Huron*, rests in the the St. Clair River bank at Port Huron's Pinegrove Park, where it is open for public inspection during scheduled hours.

(810) 982-0891

U.S.S. SILVERSIDES. Muskegon.

This battle-tested World War II submarine has been restored to the tip-top fighting condition it was in when during 14 patrols it sank 23 ships carrying 90,000 tons of materials and supplies to Japan. The 312-foot veteran of the Silent Service is open for stem-to-stern inspections of its periscopes, brass torpedo doors, sonar, sealable hatchways, klaxon (the "oogah" horn) and other hardware.

(231) 755-1230

FINEST FREIGHTER-WATCHING SPOTS

In Michigan we have an abundance of opportunities to get exciting, close-up views of 600- to 1,000-foot-long Great Lakes and ocean-going freighters, ore carriers and other cargo ships, especially from parks and other public areas along the St. Clair, Detroit and St. Mary's rivers. Following are among the best sites:

AUNE-OSBORN PARK/RIVERSIDE PARK. Sault Ste. Marie.

Vessels approaching or leaving the Soo Locks seem to brush the banks as they negotiate a sharp bend in the St. Mary's River here.

PINEGROVE PARK. Port Huron.

All downbound ships from lakes Michigan, Superior and Huron funnel through this narrow neckdown area into the St. Clair River. Added pluses here are great views of the Blue Water Bridge and a chance to walk through the museum Lightship *Huron*, a retired floating lighthouse embedded in the riverbank (p. 48).

RIVERSIDE PARK. Detroit.

An average of two dozen huge vessels per day pass in front of this wide, grassy park at the foot of Grand Boulevard practically beneath the Ambassador Bridge. And this is the only place in the world where you can watch mail and supplies be delivered "on the float" to the slowly moving behemoths by one of two 45-foot tugboat-shaped craft that zip to and from a dock next to the park. (Call 313-496-0555 for a schedule.)

SOO LOCKS. Sault Ste. Marie.

You can stand only 20 feet away from a giant "laker" or "saltie" on an elevated observation platform that overlooks the MacArthur Lock, one of four huge, gated concrete tubs that make up the largest lock system of its type in the world. Large vessels are raised and lowered the 21-foot difference between lakes Huron and Superior some 3,000 times each shipping season at an average of about one every hour and a half. A public address system announces ship names, cargo, destination and countries of origin.

ST. CLAIR BOARDWALK. St. Clair.

What's billed as "the world's longest freshwater boardwalk" — a 1,500-foot-long wood deck that edges the St. Clair River in the city of St. Clair — is an outstanding spot for close-up looks at slow-moving ships navigating one of the world's busiest shipping lanes. Coin-operated viewers bring you right on deck, and at the walkway's south end, you can combine great boat-watching with a beverage and/or meal at a restaurant/lounge whose floor-to-ceiling plate-glass windows are cantilevered almost to the river's edge.

MOST-HELPFUL, UP-TO-DATE SHIP-WATCHING GUIDE

KNOW YOUR SHIPS
(Marine Publishing Company) by Roger LeLievre

Long considered the "bible of Great Lakes boat-watching," annually updated editions include color photos plus complete vital stats on every vessel — freighters, tankers, tugs and barges — that plies the Great Lakes and St. Lawrence Seaway.

BEST STATE PARKS FOR SHIP WATCHING

ALGONAC. Algonac.

Day-use visitors and campers get long, close looks at the passing parade of ships that pass by this park's more than half mile of St. Clair River banks.
(810) 765-5605   (810) 465-2160

BRIMLEY. Brimley.

Visitors here look out at a near-continuous show of vessels moving through Lake Superior's Whitefish Bay on their way to and from the Soo Locks.
(906) 248-3422

MOST-REWARDING FREIGHTER PURSUIT

Summer evening cruises aboard the 100-passenger ferry *Isle Royale Queen III* out of Copper Harbor include tracking down and closing in on one of any freighters rounding Keweenaw Point. "Drawing up close to a big ocean-going vessel, with its six-story superstructure picked out in lights is spectacularly memorable — like something from a Fellini movie...," says *Hunts' Guide to Michigan's Upper Peninsula* (Midwestern Guides).

(906) 289-4437

BEST PLACE TO PEER AT FREIGHTERS THROUGH A PERISCOPE

DOSSIN GREAT LAKES MUSEUM. Detroit.

One of the most-popular exhibits at one of the state's finest maritime museums is a working submarine periscope that pokes up through the roof to bring cross-haired, close-up views of ship traffic moving up and down the Detroit River.

(313) 852-4051

MOST POLISHED OLD CRAFT

ANTIQUE WOODEN BOAT SHOW. Hessel.

Nearly 200 gorgeous, restored wood-hulled boats from around the country are on display for a single Saturday each August in the harbor fronting the picturesque Les Cheneaux Islands village of Hessel. The fleeting fleet of cruisers, dinghies, sculls, rowboats, canoes, yawls, sailboats, runabouts and other nautical relics has been called the finest, most-diversified public exhibit of privately owned wooden craft in the nation.

(888) 364-7526   (906) 484-9974

MOST-WATCHED HYDROPLANE RACES

SPIRIT OF DETROIT THUNDERFEST. Detroit.

During the finals of this competition for powerboat racing's coveted Gold Cup, more than half a million spectators — said to be the largest single-day crowd for a sporting event in the United States — line the Detroit River to watch the roostertails of hydroplanes skimming around a course at nearly 200 mph.

(800) 359-7760   www.thunderfest.com

WORLD-CLASS YACHT RACES

PORT HURON TO MACKINAC ISLAND

(313) 822-1853   www.byc.com

CHICAGO TO MACKINAC ISLAND

(312) 861-7777

Nearly 300 sleek sailing craft and 3,000 crew members from across North America enter each of these venerable, prestigious races, held every July. For two to three days during each event, colorful sails of 30- to 82-foot-long family cruisers, maxisleds, monohulls, multihulls and experimental designs cover courses from Port Huron and, a week later, Chicago to Mackinac Island. The 259-mile Port Huron route is rated more challenging, and the 330-mile course from Chicago is the world's longest in freshwater yachting competition.

Both races incite large, wild casting-off and sailing-in parties. Each year at Port Huron, close to 100,000 people congregate for a racing-eve send-off that resembles a mini Mardi Gras. And at the Mackinac Island finish for both races, throngs of welcomers crowd the stony harbor beach and then join crews in a two- to three-day champagne celebration that flows nonstop from the arrival of the first to last competitors, each announced by cannon shot no matter what time of day or night.

CRAFTIEST BOAT SHOW

DETROIT BOAT SHOW. Detroit.

Michigan leads the nation in the number of registered boats — more than 900,000 — and early each February nearly 15% of those boats' owners navigate to this, the state's oldest and largest all-boating consumer show. Nearly 350 exhibitors representing some 100 manufacturers unveil more than 1,000 new-model water craft including yachts, runabouts, catamarans, wave runners, sailboats, canoes, sailboards, pontoons, fishing boats, kayaks, inflatables, cabin cruisers and paddleboats.

Also helping to fill cavernous Cobo Center are displays of motors, trailers, marine equipment and accessories, and services such as financing, insuring, repair and charters.

(800) 224-3008

FISHIEST BOAT SHOW

PONTIAC SILVERDOME
BOAT, SPORT & FISHING SHOW. Pontiac.

What's billed as the largest selection of fishing boats in the state, plus tons of tackle and free advice on how to use it all are draws to this popular four-day winter exhibition. Fishermen can check out more than 400 new-model trailerable boats representing 60 makes, buy the latest hot lures at more than 100 booths, and attend free seminars conducted by respected pros and personalities who cover tactics for landing every Michigan gamefish.

(616) 530-1919

HOTTEST INDOOR FISHING HOTSPOT

Outdoor Images / Randy Correis

GREATER DETROIT SPORTFISHING & TRAVEL EXPO. Auburn Hills.

Known simply as "The Palace," this annual March show has earned a reputation as *the* place to buy both standard-issue and cutting-edge tackle and learn how to use it. The four-day event features 325 fishing-only displays and nearly 60 seminars.

(216) 529-1300

FINEST FRESHWATER FISHBOWL

BELLE ISLE AQUARIUM. Detroit.

This beautiful Pewabic-tiled, domed building holds 60 exhibit tanks filled with 32,000 gallons of water and nearly 1,500 specimens representing some 140 mostly freshwater species from around the world. The largest crowds gather around the tank holding a large electric eel that, during three-a-day feedings, generates enough current to light up lightbulbs and sound a horn.

(313) 852-4141   (248) 398-0900

BEST PLACE TO FIND MICHIGAN FISH INTERESTING and FIND INTERESTING MICHIGAN FISH

WOLF LAKE FISH HATCHERY / MICHIGAN FISHERIES INTERPRETIVE CENTER. Mattawan.

The state's largest, most-modern fish hatchery is also the most-fascinating place to learn about Michigan fish and fishing. A 7,000-square-foot interpretive building encloses 100 mounted specimens of Michigan fish, 46 record-fish plaques, a century's worth of sport-fishing tackle and lures, habitat dioramas, fish anatomy and physiology exhibits, and play-it-yourself slide shows about aquatic invaders, commercial fishing and DNR fisheries management.

Nearby you can inspect huge indoor and outdoor spawning, incubation, hatching, rearing and loading tanks and ponds that seasonally hold millions of eggs, fry and fingerlings of nearly a dozen warm- and cold-water native species for later release throughout Michigan's public waters. And from a long, wooden walkway out into a show pond, you can throw handfuls of food pellets to thrashing rainbow trout and look down through the clear water onto cruising chinook salmon, largemouth bass, and three huge, old lake sturgeon.

(616) 668-2876

MOST- COMPLEAT ANGLER GUIDES

The Fish Michigan Series (Friede Publications) by Tom Huggler

Fish Michigan—100 Southern Michigan Lakes

Fish Michigan—100 Northern Lower Michigan Lakes

Fish Michigan—100 Upper Peninsula Lakes

Fish Michigan—50 Rivers

Fish Michigan—50 More Rivers

Fish Michigan—100 Great Lakes Hotspots

Michigan's premier outdoor writer has packed these atlas-sized guidebooks with good, solid advice on where, when and how to fish the best of Michigan's vast waters. Each volume features original, large, detailed maps marked with fishing hot spots and access sites; hardcore fishing information such as year-round techniques, localized tactics, best times, and hot lures and bait; and valuable listings of bait and tackle shops, campgrounds, boat rentals, special regulations, stocking and survey records and Master Angler catches.

RATED-EXCELLENT LAKES TO DROP HOOK, LINE AND SINKER

In the inland lakes volumes of his *Fish Michigan* series, author Tom Huggler rates fishing opportunities, from poor to excellent by species, for each of 300 lakes. Only the following lakes received his top rating, an unqualified "excellent" for...

...Black Crappies
Belleville Lake. Wayne County.
Cooke Dam Pond. Iosco County. "They grow to 16 inches and it is possible to catch 100 per day."
Foote Dam Pond. Iosco County.
Fremont Lake. Newaygo County.

...Bluegills
Cooke Dam Pond. Iosco County.
Foote Dam Pond. Iosco County.
Lake Chemung. Livingston County.
Patterson Lake. Livingston County.
Silver Lake. Branch County.

...Channel Catfish
Lake Charlevoix. Charlevoix County. "Michigan's third-largest lake...produces monster catfish."
Mott Lake. Genesee County.

...Largemouth Bass
Gull Lake. Kalamazoo County. "...popular with bass fishing clubs, which often hold tournaments there."
Lake Orion. Oakland County. "... bass are so large and healthy."

...Northern Pike
Big Platte Lake. Benzie County.

...Redear Sunfish
Silver Lake. Branch County.

...Rock Bass
Gull Lake. Kalamazoo County.

...Smallmouth Bass
Big Platte Lake. Benzie County. "...contains a hefty population...with lunkers from 5 to 6 pounds...available."
Deer Island Lake. Gogebic.
Douglas Lake. Cheboygan County.
Green Lake. Grand Traverse County.
Lake Charlevoix. Charlevoix County.

...Walleyes
Black Lake. Cheboygan County.
Fremont Lake. Newaygo County.
Gun Lake. Barry County. "...some of the best walleye fishing in southern Michigan... ."
South Lake Leelanau. Leelanau County. "Walleye...anglers regularly rate it among the top ten in Michigan.
Sunset Lake. Iron County.
Woodard Lake. Ionia County.

...Yellow Perch
Cooke Dam Pond. Iosco County.
Foote Dam Pond. Iosco County.
Sunset Lake. Iron County.

MOST OUTSTANDING FISHING LAKE

MUSKEGON LAKE. Muskegon.

Of 300 inland lakes covered in his *Fish Michigan* series, author Tom Huggler singles out Muskegon as being the only one to offer *outstanding* fishing opportunities for a wide variety of warmwater gamefish, especially walleyes, yellow perch, flathead catfish and smallmouth bass. A drowned rivermouth that also hosts transient trout and salmon in spring and fall, "Muskegon...could make a valid claim as the state's best fishing lake," writes Huggler.

ALMOST HEINZ-57 LAKE

GULL LAKE. Kalamazoo.

This large, clean, deep lake holds 52 fish species, more than any other of Michigan's 11,000 inland lakes.

MOST-COMFORTABLE RIVER-FISHING SPOT

FALLING WATERS LODGE. Leland.

This 21-room 3-story motel motel sits only feet from the Carp River near where it dumps into Lake Michigan, and guests staying in streamside rooms often toss lures into the water from their patios and balconies.

(231) 256-9832

MOST-POPULAR SMELT-DIPPING PARTY

SINGING BRIDGE. Au Gres.

In April when TV or radio announcers sound the call that smelt are running at the mouth of the East Branch Au Gres River, hordes of mid-Michigan dippers also make after-midnight runs to the area. There, jammed net to long-handled net, the festive smelters dip furiously for the minnow-size fish and then stagger away with, though not necessarily because of, full buckets.

MOST CONTAINED WORMS

D.M.F. BAIT CO. (Waterford) claims to be the world's largest wholesale packaged-bait dealer. During the fishing season they package and ship more than 60 million nightcrawlers to customers, including Wal-Mart and Kmart, in 49 states.

RATED-EXCELLENT FISHING RIVERS

In *Fish Michigan — 50 Rivers* and *Fish Michigan — 50 More Rivers* author Tom Huggler rates fishing opportunities, from poor to excellent by species, for each of 100 streams. Only the following received his top rating, an unqualified "excellent" for...

...BROOK TROUT
Black River. Cheboygan County.
Two Hearted River
White River. Muskegon and Newaygo counties.

...BROWN TROUT
White River. Muskegon and Newaygo counties.

...LARGEMOUTH BASS
Detroit River

...RAINBOW TROUT
Two Hearted River

...ROCK BASS
Kalamazoo River

...SMALLMOUTH BASS
Detroit River
Kalamazoo River
Menominee River
St. Joseph River

...SMELT
Black River. near Harrisville.
Days River
East Branch Au Gres River

...WALLEYES
Detroit River
Kalamazoo River
Saginaw River
Tittabawassee River

Outdoor Images / Randy Comels

WHEN NATURE CALLS

MOST NATURAL GETAWAYS GUIDE

NATURAL MICHIGAN
(Friede Publications) by Tom Powers

This exhaustive, comprehensive volume describes outstanding scenery and opportunities to birdwatch, hike, cross country ski, camp, picnic, swim and find flora and fauna at a whopping 228 natural areas.

RAREST STAIRMASTER NATURE STUDY

STAIRWAY TO DISCOVERY. Oscoda.

"(This) is the most unusual interpretive nature trail in Michigan," says *Natural Michigan* (Friede Publications) author Tom Powers, "... and may be the only trail in the U.S. perched in its entirety on a staircase." Two hundred sixty steps descend to the edge of the Au Sable River, with signs at 10 stops explaining the natural history of the surrounding River Road National Forest Scenic Byway area.

BEST NATURE CENTER

CHIPPEWA NATURE CENTER. Midland.

All the experts agree on this one. Tom Powers, for instance, in *Natural Michigan* (Friede Publications) calls Chippewa "the 'Cadillac' of Michigan nature centers. *Hunts' Highlights of Michigan* (Midwestern Guides) says that it "clearly stands out from the rest of Michigan's many fine nature centers." And a vice-president of the National Audubon Society labeled Chippewa "one of the finest — if not *the* finest — private nature centers in the *world.*"

The visitor center, designed by Michigan's first Architect Laureate, features a glass-walled room that juts out over the Pine River, with views downstream to where it joins the Chippewa River. Also inside are a museum, nature art, 50 custom-made exhibits, an auditorium, a library, classrooms and a gift shop.

Outside, 14 miles of trails cut through nearly 1,000 acres of diverse habitat that takes in three miles of river frontage, archaeological sites, a man-made wetlands, a log homestead, and an arboretum of Michigan trees.

(517) 631-0830   www.chippewanaturecenter.com

BEST BOOK TO SEE THE TREES FOR THE FOREST

MICHIGAN TREES
(University of Michigan Press) by Burton V. Barnes and Warren H. Wagner, Jr.

This amply illustrated guide is authoritative and complete enough to be used by several universities as a textbook yet user-friendly enough to help to casual and amateur naturalists identify hundreds of different Michigan trees by their leaves, fruits, flowers, bark and nuts.

MOST-TREMENDOUS TREES

•The largest American elm in the United States towers 112 feet over a pig farm near Buckley. The 300-year-old tree's 23.5-foot base girth splits into two dozen smaller trunks that open up into a 115-wide canopy.

•On South Manitou Island in a stand of virgin white cedar known as the Valley of the Giants stands a 500-year-old world-record specimen measuring 111 feet high and 17½ feet around.

•The largest known living specimen of Michigan's state tree — a 200-year-old white pine growing in Porcupine Mountains Wilderness State Park — measures 200 inches around and about 150 feet high.

•The world's largest number of trees that produce one of the world's rarest woods, bird's-eye maple, grow in the western Upper Peninsula, particularly the Keweenaw area. Single logs of the beautiful tight-knotted, swirl-grained hardwood can sell for several thousand dollars.

GREATEST GLASS TREE HOUSE

LENA MEIJER CONSERVATORY. Grand Rapids.
Michigan's newest and largest tropical conservatory — a 5-story-tall, 15,000-square-foot giant greenhouse — holds 2,000 tropical plants representing 300 species from five continents.
(616) 957-1580   www.meijergardens.org

BEST PLACE TO SEE THE TREES WITHOUT THE FOREST

NICHOLS ARBORETUM. Ann Arbor.
An arboretum, according to the Random House dictionary, is "a plot of land on which many different trees or shrubs are grown for study or display." Michigan's finest example is Nichols Arboretum, a collection of more than 500 varieties of exotic and native trees and shrubs spread in both formal and natural settings over 123 acres of diverse landscape at the edge of the University of Michigan campus. Walking-tour brochures, available at UM's School of Natural Resources and Environment, help identify some plantings.
(734) 998-7175

GREATEST GARDEN

BEAL BOTANICAL GARDEN. East Lansing.
The nation's oldest, and the state's best botanical garden is tended by horticulturists at the nation's oldest agricultural college, Michigan State University. Hundreds of beds, neatly crammed into just five acres, hold more than 5,000 different species of vegetation from around the world, from common weeds to endangered species to exotic pharmaceutical plants to rare hybrids.
(517) 355-7750

MOST-SPECTACULAR FORMAL BACK-YARD GARDEN

CRANBROOK GARDENS. Bloomfield Hills.
The Cranbrook Estate, built in 1908 by newspaper mogul George C. Booth, includes a back yard like no other in Michigan. The 325-acre site, now maintained by the Cranbrook Institute, takes in 100 species of trees, a greenhouse, a promenade with reflecting pool, sculptures, fountains, and dozens of specialty planting areas such as the Kitchen, Oriental, Sundial and Sunken gardens. Twelve-foot-high fieldstone walls surround the formal gardens, and any of the open, sunny spaces not covered by manicured grass are annually filled with thousands of flowers.
(248) 645-3149

MOST-EXPANSIVE, EXTENSIVE INFORMAL BACK-YARD GARDEN

DOW GARDENS. Midland.

Begun in 1899 as the back-yard hobby of the founder of the Dow Chemical Corporation, this 110-acre former pine plantation has been metamorphasized into one of the finest overall collection of plants in the country. Michigan's most-uniquely beautiful garden now comprises a stunning variety, number and range of plants including

- some 1,200 different woody trees and shrubs, including more than 105 different kinds of flowering crab apple trees
- 500 different perennials, wildflowers and ground covers
- an herb garden
- a rose garden
- 25,000 tulips
- 15,000 annuals representing more than 450 varieties
- 10,000 bedding plants.

The plantings are accented by hidden pools, massive boulders, a creek and waterfalls and are subtly connected by paved paths with stepping stones and small footbridges that cross the creek.

(800) 362-4874   www.dowgardens.org

BEST PLACE TO STOP AND SMELL THE CONEFLOWERS

PURPLE CONEFLOWER PLANT PRESERVE. Moran.

A 21-acre clearing just off M-123 halfway between Moran and Trout Lake is the only place in Michigan where the purple coneflower grows, even though it shouldn't. The plant thrives in the soft, rich soil of its native Great Plains states, but it shouldn't survive the poor, rocky soil and harsh winters of the Upper Peninsula. Yet late each summer its large, beautiful royal-purple, daisy-like blooms reappear to cover the site of the ghost town of Kenneth.

MOST KID-FRIENDLY PLOTS

MICHIGAN 4-H GARDEN.
Michigan State University, East Lansing.

The first garden in the country designed exclusively for children includes an arched span bridge over a water garden, a leapfrog fountain, a maze, and a climb-through Tree House, all placed among 55 minigardens with child-appeal names such as Pizza, Cereal, Alphabet, Alice-in-Wonderland, Maze, and Dinosaur.

(517) 353-4800   (517) 355-0348

TOP-RATED FLOWER AND GARDEN SHOW

ANN ARBOR FLOWER AND GARDEN SHOW. Ann Arbor.

Cutting-edge model gardens; seminars, forums and free advice; demonstrations and displays; a limited number of carefully selected vendors offering the best in garden sculpture, supplies and accessories; and of course hundreds of varieties of live plants and shrubs are reasons this annual late-March, four-day-long show rates among the top 10 in the nation.

(734) 434-8004

MOST-EXHAUSTIVE PETAL PUSHER

MICHIGAN WILDFLOWERS IN COLOR
(Thunder Bay Press) by Harry C. Lund

This incredibly complete, beautiful work features a color photo plus detailed description — including scientific and family name, physical characteristics, habitats and season of growth — for each of more than 275 different kinds of wildflowers that grow in Michigan.

BEST BOOK FOR CULTIVATING PLOTS

MICHIGAN GARDENING GUIDE
(University of Michigan Press) by Jerry Minnich

From this guide, casual to serious horticulturists can unearth a wealth of detailed directions and practical tips for successfully growing vegetables, herbs, landscaping plants, flowers and house plants in Michigan's varying soil types and potentially frustrating climate.

GREATEST GUINNESS GROWTHS

A 3-lb., 2-oz. apple grown in Caro by the Miklovic family in 1992 and a 36-lb. kohlrabi raised in 1979 by Emil Krejci of Mt. Clemens are, as of 1999, still listed in the *Guinness Book of World Records* (Guinness Media, Inc.) as all-time largests.

RAREST RARE-BULB RETAILER

OLD HOUSE GARDENS. Ann Arbor.

North America's only specialists in antique, heirloom bulbs offer rare, unusual, and vanishing domestic and foreign varieties for sale by mail. Their fascinating catalog listing of plants that have grown in gardens from 1200 AD to the 1950s includes the world's oldest named dahlia and a distinctive daffodil discovered shortly after the turn of the century on an isolated English Isles sea cliff.

(734) 995-1486 www.oldhousegardens.com

MOST-PERVASIVE FUNGUS

In 1992 scientists discovered that edible "honey mushrooms" that sprout along the Michigan-Wisconsin border each fall were the above-ground shoots of a huge, single fungus that has spread underground from a single spore for more than 1,500 years. The humongous fungus — estimated to cover 37 acres and weigh 110 tons — is the world's second-largest living organism, according to *Audubon Magazine*.

MOST-EFFICIENT VIRTUAL MANURE SPREADER

MICHIGAN MANURE RESOURCES NETWORK. Ottawa County.

To help even out gluts and shortages of animal-waste farm fertilizer around the state, the Michigan State University Extension Service set up this unusual website — http://web2.canr.msu.edu/manure/ — as an internet brokerage barn for the odiferous commodity. Farmers from all Michigan counties can log on and then log in their phone numbers, addresses, and type and quality of manure they have for sale or want to purchase.

MOST-UNIQUE NONSEASONAL USE OF SNOW-REMOVAL EQUIPMENT

Summer mayfly hatches are so heavy in the LaPlaisance Bay (Lake Erie) area, according to Tom Huggler in his *Fish Michigan — 100 Great Lakes Hotspots*, that "managers at Toledo Beach Marina use a snowplow to remove the insects from parking lots and sidewalks."

Nearby, down the coast in Luna Pier, street sweepers are used to clear I-75.

MOST-DETAILED LIST OF A FAT-CAT STALKER'S VICTIMS

Over an 18-month period during the late 1940s, the Rose Lake Wildlife Experiment Station (East Lansing) manager kept a log of all the prey his house cat proudly presented to him. They were 1,200 meadow mice; 400 house, deer and jumping mice; 554 English sparrows; 15 barn rats; six meadowlarks; four rabbits; three 13-lined spermophiles; one flicker and one robin.

WILDEST TRAFFIC-FATALITY STUDY

Ionia County is the only Michigan county ever to have officially counted animals flattened on its roads. During 1971 (the one and only survey year) 445 raccoons, 163 squirrels, 140 turtles, 137 opossums, 82 skunks, 77 deer, 67 cats, 66 dogs, 57 woodchucks, 49 muskrats, 45 rabbits, 22 fox and 16 pheasants were splattered over the county's 114 miles of highways.

EASIEST ACCESS TO ANIMAL AFTERLIFE

PETNET MEMORIAL PARK
HTTP://PETNET.DETNEWS.COM/

Animal lovers can lay deceased pets to virtual rest in this unique cybercemetery. To inter a furry, feathered or scaled friend, the owner enters the pet's name and a personalized eulogy, then creates a customized memorial web page by selecting from a variety of type styles and backgrounds. A virtual granite tombstone engraved with the animal's name then appears on screen with others along separate garden pathways for Rabbits and Rodents, Fish and Exotic Pets, Dogs, Cats, and Horses and Birds. Visitors can scroll down the lanes and pay respects by calling up the written tributes with mouse clicks on the tombstones.

BEST PLACE TO COMMISERATE WITH CONVALESCING WILDLIFE

HOWELL NATURE CENTER. Howell.

During scheduled visiting hours, humans can extend well wishes to a menagerie of patients being cared for at this unique National Wildlife Rehabilitation Association-licensed facility. Each year more than 1,000 orphaned, sick, injured and confiscated birds and animals representing approximately 50 different common and exotic species are admitted, treated and most often released back into the wild.

(517) 546-0249   www.ismi.net/howellnature

MOST-EDUCATIONAL SPECIAL DELIVERIES

MICHIGAN STATE FAIR. Detroit.

Each year thousands of wide-eyed children, their parents and other adults witness and often cheer the arrival into the world of a hundred or so pigs, sheep, cows and other animals at the annual state fair's Miracle of Life animal-birthing exhibit. Animals are brought into the exhibit area a few days before their due date and are monitored throughout the process by Michigan State University College of Veterinary Medicine students and staff.

(313) 369-8250

BEST ZOO

DETROIT ZOOLOGICAL PARK. Royal Oak.

This 125-acre mixture of finger-pointing, camera-clicking opportunities plus interactive education ranks as one of Michigan's top-six attractions and one of the country's top-10 zoos. Annually, more than a million visitors view some 1,300 specimens representing 250 species in indoor settings and barless, moated, natural-looking outdoor habitats. Included is the world's best chimpanzee exhibit and nationally renowned penguin, bird, bear, reptile and amphibian collections. And slated for a year-2000 opening is a 4-acre, $13 million polar bear exhibit that promises to be the world's largest and most realistic.

(248) 398-0900   www.detroitzoo.org

BEST PLACE TO GO TO THE DOGS

DETROIT KENNEL CLUB DOG SHOW. Detroit.

More than 3,000 dogs representing an incredible 149 breeds sit for up-close inspection by judges and prospective pet owners at North America's largest benched canine show. For seven hours a day during the two-day affair each spring, potential best-of-breeds from Affenpinschers to Yorkshire terrriers obediently perch on benches while 80,000 showgoers unleash upon breeders/handlers dogged questions about the animals' temperaments, grooming, health and training.

(248) 352-7469

BUSIEST BEAVERS

One-mile-long Echo Lake, near the center of Grand Island offshore from Munising, is the largest beaver-created pond in the world, according to *Natural Michigan* (Friede Publications).

MOST-USED HANGOUTS

CHAPIN MINE. Iron Mountain.

Late each fall, more than a million brown bats arrive in the Iron Mountain area, where they hang around — from ledges, awnings, soffits and other projections — until cold weather kills off their insect food supply. One of the world's largest gathering of bats then swarms to the abandoned Chapin underground iron mine, where they hibernate. When weather warms in the spring, the bats reverse their route but get out of town quickly.

TIPPY DAM. Wellston.

The chambers below this dam's spillway make up the Lower Peninsula's only known bat hibernaculum, which provides winter shelter to more than 20,000 of the flying, insect-devouring mammals.

CHOICEST GUIDE TO ANIMAL PHOTO SHOOTS

MICHIGAN WILDLIFE VIEWING GUIDE
(Michigan State University Press)
DNR Natural Heritage Program

A statewide committee of experts chose 121 of the state's best spots to view and photograph a variety of Michigan wildlife from bats to wood ducks. Details for featured sites include color photos, short descriptions, maps and directions.

MOST-INDULGENT WAY TO VIEW WILD ELK

Horse-drawn wagons or, in winter, sleighs transport guests at the Thunder Bay Resort in Hillman to prime, private elk-viewing areas. The up-close, lengthy looks at the majestic animals are followed by a five-course gourmet dinner at a rustic cabin located deep in the woods on a scenic double bend of the Thunder Bay River.

(800) 729-9375   www.thunderbaygolf.com

BEST TIMES AND PLACES TO OBSERVE WILD ELK

More than 1,000 wild elk, the largest herd east of the Mississippi, concentrate in the 98,000-acre Pigeon River Country State Forest east of Gaylord and Vanderbilt. There, several designated and informal viewing areas offer good to excellent chances of spotting the magnificent, imposing animals, some racked with tremendous antlers. Early morning and the hour before sunset are the best times to catch elk in the open, and you greatly improve your odds by bringing binoculars during the month-long rutting season, which generally begins early to mid-September. Not only can you see the animals then but also hear 750-pound bulls attract cow harems and ward off competing males with a wild assortment of wheezes, whistles and intimidating grunts known as bugling.

Three easy-to-get-to good viewing areas, with parking spots that overlook fields the DNR plants with elk-attracting crops, are located

- •3.5 miles east of Vanderbilt on Sturgeon Valley Rd. to Fontinalis Rd. then 3 miles north on Fontinalis.

- •8.5 miles east of Vanderbilt on Sturgeon Valley Rd. almost to the Pigeon River.

- •11.5 miles east of Vanderbilt on Sturgeon Valley Rd. to Twin Lakes Rd. then 2 miles north then east on Twin Lakes to Osmun Rd. then north on Osmun 4.5 miles to Clark Bridge Rd.

All three locations are among several marked on maps/brochures available from the Gaylord & Convention & Visitors Bureau (800) 345-8621, Atlanta Chamber of Commerce (517) 785-3400, and at DNR offices in Atlanta and Gaylord. For the most current elk-watch updates and helpful advice, contact the DNR Pigeon River ranger station at (517) 732-3541.

BEST PLACE TO LET SLEEPING RATTLERS LIE

SKEGEMOG SWAMP PATHWAY. Kalkaska.

During warm-weather months here, secretive, poisonous Massasauga rattlesnakes commonly slither from their hiding places onto a sun-baked, abandoned railroad grade, according to the *Michigan Wildlife Viewing Guide* (Michigan State University Press). And though the small snake is not known to be aggressive, the authors advise observing it "from a healthy distance and count(ing) yourself as one of the lucky few who ever see Michigan's only rattlesnake."

(231) 929-7911   (231) 258-2711

BEST PLACES TO WATCH BUTTERFLIES FLUTTER BY

FREDERIK MEIJER GARDENS. Grand Rapids.

During what's called the country's largest temporary butterfly exhibit, hundreds of tropical and native farm-raised butterflies are released to dart and glide throughout the Lena Meijer Conservatory for three weeks each spring.

(616) 957-1580   www.meijergardens.org

MACKINAC ISLAND BUTTERFLY HOUSE. Mackinac Island.

In this greenhouse on McGulpin Street more than 500 colorful butterflies representing 30 species and replenished at 350 per week feast on cabbage, fennel and other butterfly food from Memorial Day to Labor Day. Butterflies and visitors are at peak activity during July and August.

(906) 847-3972

WINGS OF MACKINAW. Mackinaw City.

As many as 500 native and exotic butterflies are released weekly during the summer to flutter and float through a specially designed solarium attached to this gift shop. Visitors rest on benches here; butterflies often rest on visitors.

(231) 436-7372

BEST PLACE TO SEE SQUIRRELS SOAR

FORT WILKINS STATE PARK. Copper Harbor.

It's uncommon to see one of the state's most-common mammals, the flying squirrel, because the shy, big-eyed mammal is almost exclusively nocturnal. The best chance of watching the furry aerobats, according to the *Michigan Wildlife Viewing Guide* (Michigan State University Press), comes at dusk at the east campground of Ft. Wilkins State Park where good numbers of the small squirrels "scamper up (large red pines) and launch themselves into gentle glides between trees."

(906) 289-4215

MOST-RESURRECTED SWAMP

SENEY WILDLIFE REFUGE. Seney.

Originally part of a vast area known as the Great Manistique Swamp, this Upper Peninsula tract was logged and burned by lumbermen then drained and abandoned by developers. But beginning during the Depression, workers from the Civilian Conservation Corps and other state and federal agencies gradually reconstructed, rehabilitated, restored and re-created a 95,000-acre wildlife refuge that is now home to more than 200 species of birds and 50 species of mammals. The outstanding project also created one of the best places in the state for humans — from a car or bike or on foot — to see a wide range of wildlife in their natural surroundings.

(906) 586-9851

The leading authority on Michigan's best birdwatching sites is Tom Powers, author of *Great Birding in the Great Lakes: A Guide to the 50 Best Birdwatching Sites in the Great Lakes States* (Walloon Press) and *Natural Michigan* (Friede Publications). The following birdwatching bests, including quotes, has been compiled from those two books.

BEST ALL-AROUND BIRDING SPOTS

METRO BEACH METROPARK. Mt. Clemens.

"Extensive marshes, open water and woods..., plus the park's location on a major bird migration route are reasons that 260 species — some in large concentrations and 80 of which have nested here — have been spotted." The area's field checklist includes a sampling of nearly every bird family.

(810) 463-4332

TAWAS POINT STATE PARK. East Tawas.

"(This) peninsula is one of the finest collectors of (migrating) birds in the Midwest, and (its) tip...concentrates them like the small end of a funnel. Tawas Point State Park boasts more than 250 species on its checklist, and it often seems that most, if not all, of these species can be seen, at one time or another, on or from the last 100 feet of the peninsula."

(517) 362-5041

BEST PLACE TO WATCH...

... GYRFALCON
SAULTE STE. MARIE.

A lone representative of the largest of all falcons, a species rarely spotted in the U.S., overwinters at the Soo and spends mornings and evenings perched on the window ledges or cupola of the Edison Power Plant at the edge of the St. Mary's River.

(705) 256-2790

...HAWKS (includes eagles, falcons, vultures and true hawks)
LAKE ERIE METROPARK. Rockwood.

"...one of the three best hawk-watching sites in North America, and in numbers counted it is the top spot east of the Mississippi. And...we are talking about incredible, unbelievable, staggering numbers. ...228,000 Broad-winged Hawks seen in one day, ...56,000 counted in one hour, and 25,000 tallied in 15 minutes."

(800) 477-3189

..KIRTLAND'S WARBLER
GRAYLING AND MIO.

The only breeding grounds in the world for one of the world's rarest birds, the Kirtland's Warbler, are managed jack pine forests in northern Michigan. From mid-May through early July, U.S. Fish & Wildlife Service and Michigan DNR personnel lead groups of novice and experienced birders from around the globe on free guided tours into the nesting areas for possible glimpses of the ½-oz, bluish-gray bird.

(517) 351-2555 and (517) 826-3252

...OWLS

WHITEFISH POINT. Paradise.
"...one of the best owl-watching locations in the country... ."
(906) 492-3596

...SANDHILL CRANES
HAEHNLE MEMORIAL SANCTUARY. Jackson.

As many as 2,000 representatives of America's third-largest bird, some standing four feet high with wing spans over six feet, stop at this marshy sanctuary during spring and fall migrations.

...SHOREBIRDS (such as terns, gulls, heron, egrets, sandpipers, plovers, and dowitchers)
POINTE MOUILLEE STATE GAME AREA. Rockwood.

This huge complex of wetlands, diked marshes, river bayous, and a 3-mile-long man-made barrier island "... is undoubtedly the finest shorebird viewing area in Michigan and one of the best in the Midwest. ...More than 250 species have been recorded...and the list includes birds you have little or no chance of seeing anywhere else in the Midwest."

BEST PLACE TO GET A BIRD'S-EYE VIEW OF BIRDS

BROCKWAY MOUNTAIN DRIVE. Copper Harbor.

Drafts created by cliffs that edge Michigan's highest roadway (p. 29) attract migrating hawks that ride the rising air as they pass through the area. Many of the soaring birds are below the cliff top, so observers have the unique opportunity to look down on them.

(906) 482-2388

CLOSEST ENCOUNTERS WITH AVIAN PREDATORS

KELLOGG BIRD SANCTUARY. Augusta.

Outdoor flight cages at this beautiful refuge hold one of the Midwest's largest collections of birds of prey — such as hawks, owls and eagles — that, because of injury or because they were raised as pets, can no longer survive in the wild.

(616) 671-2510

BEST CRAPPY PLACE TO BIRDWATCH

MUSKEGON WASTEWATER TREATMENT AREA. Muskegon.

This sprawling sewage-treatment plant complex, says Tom Powers in *Natural Michigan* (Friede Publications), is "one of the state's great birdwatching areas, a place where...you can, with little effort, observe a staggering number of birds rare to Michigan. ...Extensive fields, shallow lagoons, dikes and small woodlots...draw an enormous number and variety of birds... ."

BEST PLACES TO HEAR SAND CONCERTS

GRAND HAVEN AND P.J. HOFFMASTER STATE PARKS. Grand Haven.

The beaches here are among only a few in the world where the sand's unique silky consistency causes it to squeak when walked on. Some have even described the characteristic sound as a recognizable musical note or whistle and the phenomena as "singing sand."

(616) 842-4910

BEST PLACES TO LEAVE NO STONE UNTURNED

Finding a choice agate quickens the pulse of even a casual beachcomber. The variegated, banded remainders of ancient volcanic activity, polished smooth by water and sand over thousands of years, are colorful and captivating. Most-prized are Lake Superior agates, which are plentiful at two prime spots:

AGATE BEACH. Copper Harbor.

A trail from the Copper Harbor Marina leads to a section of Lake Superior shoreline strewn with thousands of agates. However, they're not easy to spot, as they are mixed in with millions of other "ordinary" stones and pebbles. Fresh batches of agates appear at ice-out in spring and after storms, and it's easiest to see their red, brown, white or clear markings on cloudy, overcast days. When the sky is sunny, experienced agate hunters say to look into shallow, clear water or where waves wet the rocky shore.

AGATE BEACH. Grand Marais.

A short path from a parking area off H-58 just north of the Pictured Rocks National Lakeshore drops past picturesque Sable Falls to the Lake Superior shore. From there to about a mile east, shallow-water areas plus where beach meets banks can be rife with agates obvious even to rookie rockhunters.

STANDOUT SITES TO SEARCH FOR THE STATE STONE

The Petoskey stone, Michigan's official rock, is actually petrified coral that lived in a salt-water sea that covered Michigan 350 million years ago. The fossil's characteristic gray-green, white-bordered hexagonal markings can only be seen when wet, so successful hunters dodge waves at the water's edge, wade out into shallow areas, and even search shores in the rain. Spring ice-out and major fall storms wash in fresh specimens, which range from thumbnail- to boulder-size. Petoskey Stones are most-commonly found along northwest Michigan's Great Lakes coastline, with the following being especially and consistently good spots:

BAYFRONT PARK & MAGNUS CITY PARK. Petoskey.

FISHERMAN'S ISLAND STATE PARK. Charlevoix.

LEELANAU STATE PARK. Northport.

PETERSON PARK. Northport.

BEST ROCK COLLECTION

A.E. SEAMAN MINERALOGICAL MUSEUM.
Michigan Technological University, Houghton.

"The only geology museum that's clearly better than ours is Harvard's," one Michigan Tech faculty member has reportedly said in rating his school's sparkling collection of more than 19,000 minerals and rock specimens from around the world. Expert, some say artful, displays on the formation and uses of minerals include fluorescent specimens highlighted by black lights, a cave simulating an iron mine, and pieces of volcanic "bombs" from the Mt. St. Helens, Washington, eruption.

(906) 487-2572

HEAVIEST HEAVENLY IMPACT

Accompanied by thunderous rumbling sounds, a 70-pound meteorite crashed into the streets of Allegan on July 10, 1889, with such force that it buried itself 1½ feet in the ground.

GRANDEST CANYON

STURGEON RIVER GORGE. Sidnaw.

Over the centuries the fast, powerful Sturgeon River has gouged a section of Upper Peninsula wilderness into a 250- to 400-foot-deep, ½- to 1-mile wide canyon, the largest and deepest in the Great Lakes states.

BIGGEST CAVITY

BEAR CAVE. Buchanan.

Michigan's largest natural cave, though small by geologic standards, does feature interesting standard-issue formations such as stalactites, stalagmites, petrified leaves, fossils and flowstone. A nominal admission fee includes a 20-minute audiotape that guides visitors on a paved walkway through the 150-foot-long, 15-foot-tall (at its highest) tunnel-like chamber eroded out of 25,000-year-old limestone directly under the St. Joseph River.

(616) 695-3050

GREATEST SHAKES

Because Michigan rests on a solid rock base, few naturally occurring earthquakes have shaken the state, and most of those have been shockwaves from "seismic disturbances" centered elsewhere. The most-dramatic of those struck in December 1811 when one in the series of New Madrid Earthquakes, which measured an incredible 8.5 on the Richter scale, reached out of the Mississippi Valley into Michigan. The tremendous shock apparently caused the Mississippi River to briefly flow backwards, and in southern Michigan, judge James Witherell reported that the tremor caused Orchard Lake to roil, sending to shore large numbers of turtles, which local Indians collected and ate.

Most recently — on July 27, 1980, at 2:54 p.m. — the upper tail of a quake centered in Kentucky rumbled through southern Michigan, rocking buildings, breaking dishes and windows, and during the fifth inning of a baseball game, causing the top levels of Tiger Stadium to sway noticeably.

The largest of the only two verified earthquakes that have originated in Michigan took place at 9:47 p.m. on August 9, 1947, when a one-minute quake centered at Coldwater rattled windows, moved furnishings and toppled the chimneys of buildings from Benton Harbor to Detroit and from Adrian to Saginaw.

EXPRESSIONS

MOST-UNIQUE HIGH SCHOOL NICKNAMES

The overwhelming majority of the Michigan High School Athletic Association's 728 member schools have adopted common nicknames, particularly animals (e.g., panthers, cougars, tigers, wolves, huskies) and birds (e.g., falcons, cardinals, hawks, eagles).

Following are the farthest departures from tradition.

BATTLING BATHERS. Mt. Clemens.

CHIX. Zeeland.

COSMOS. Hamtramck.

FLIVVERS. Kingsford.

GREMLINS. Houghton.

HATCHETS. Bad Axe.

HEMATITES. Ishpeming.

JUNGALEERS. Detroit Southeastern.

MARTIANS. Goodrich.

MAJI. Colon.

RIVER RATS. Ann Arbor Huron.

ROCKS. Canton Plymouth Salem.

SADDLELITES. Harper Woods Regina.

TRACTORS. Dearborn.

STRAIGHTEST SOURCE OF GAY PRIDE

Near the turn of the 20th century, a small copper-smelting community on the Keweenaw Peninsula's south shore named itself after mining company director Joseph Gay. Today, about all that remains in the isolated near-ghost town is its tavern, The Gay Bar, which still serves area residents, plays it straight with occasional prank callers, and sells T-shirts to tourists.

MOST-UNPRETENTIOUS, ALLITERATIVE SPORTS TEAM NAME

LANSING LUGNUTS, Class A Chicago Cubs affiliate minor-league baseball team.

CLASSIEST WAY TO CANCEL CHRISTMAS

To add a unique touch to your Christmas holiday greetings, place your stamped cards and letters in one package and send it to the postmaster at any of the following towns, along with a note requesting that your mail be cancelled with their postmark.

CHRISTMAS (49862)

HOLLY (48442)

NAZARETH (49074)

MOST SCENT-SATIONAL PHONE LISTINGS

The 1999 Ameritech Traverse City "let your fingers do the walking" publication included a National Cherry Festival ad featuring images of the fruit that, when scratched, gave off a cherry aroma. An Ameritech official speculated that their scratch-and-sniff telephone directory was the country's first.

MOST-PROVOCATIVE MAP ALTERATION

On Michigan's official 1978 Department of Transportation highway map, the agency's chairman, an obviously enthusiastic University of Michigan athletic supporter, added the following two towns to the section of Ohio that appeared south of Michigan's border — goblu and beatosu.

MOST-UNUSUAL PLACE-NAME ORIGINS

COLON

Early settlers agreed to a quick, uncomplicated way to name their community. One randomly flipped open a dictionary, another dropped his finger onto the definition of the body part and, according to Walter Romig in *Michigan Place Names* (Wayne State University Press) stated "We *will* call it Colon, for the lake and the river (here) correspond exactly to the shape of a colon."

FENTON

When Dibbleville's three largest landholders decided to change their settlement's name in 1837, local lore has it that they held a poker game. William Fenton won the first hand and rights to name the town after himself. The two main streets were then named after the losers, Robert Leroy and Norman Rockwell. The game continued, with the winners of subsequent hands naming the town's streets after family members.

GERMFASK

This town's name, according to Walter Romig in *Michigan Place Names* (Wayne State University Press), was made up from the surname initials of the eight founding settlers: *G*rant, *E*dge, *R*obinson, *M*ead, *F*rench, *A*ckley, *S*hepard, and *K*naggs.

MOST-MERCIFUL NAME CHANGES

CATHOLEPISTIMIAD TO UNIVERSITY OF MICHIGAN
 Otherwise, sports announcers would have broken their mouths.

BAGLEY'S CORNERS TO BLOOMFIELD HILLS
 "Bagley's Corners Cranbrook" just doesn't have the same upscale ring to it.

RATTLESNAKE ISLAND TO HOG ISLAND TO BELLE ISLE

BEST-KNOWN PSEUDONYMOUS RIVER

TWO HEARTED RIVER. Luce County.
 This Upper Peninsula stream became nationally known after Ernest Hemingway used its name in his short story, "Big Two Hearted River." However, the river Hemingway actually described through his character Nick Adams was the nearby, unpoetic-sounding Fox.

MOST NOVEL BAR BULLETS

Still lodged in the wood bar of Big Bay's Lumberjack Tavern are bullets fired in 1952 during the real-life killing that inspired the best-selling novel and movie *Anatomy of a Murder*.

MOST-SELECT PLACE TO CREATE X-FILES

CLARION SCIENCE FICTION
AND FANTASY WRITERS' WORKSHOP. East Lansing.
 One of the nation's most-prestigious and best-known writers' workshops is an intensive and intense 41-day regimen of sessions conducted by some of the country's best science-fiction writers. Manuscript critiques have a reputation for being so brutally candid that the 20 students annually admitted to the MSU-sponsored summer course pass around a stuffed blue "comfort bunny."

(517) 355-9598   www.msu.edu/~lbs/clarion/select.html

BEST WORST-VERSE CONTEST

JULIA A. MOORE POETRY CONTEST. Flint.
 The winner of this unusual annual competition, sponsored by the Flint Public Library, is honored as the worst poet in the state. The contest is named after Julia A. Moore, a Grand Rapids woman who earned derisive fame by publishing painfully awful, unintentionally funny verse in the 1870s.

Almost all of the hundreds of entries mimic Moore's forced rhyme and meter and inappropriate word usage. And many — such as a finalist who lamented the death of a girl who suffocated in a manure pile — follow Moore's penchant for morbid themes, poetically treating bodily functions, body parts, death and degradation.

(810) 232-7111

MOST-ARRESTING LANGUAGE POLICE

LAKE SUPERIOR STATE UNIVERSITY. Sault Ste. Marie.

Michigan's smallest public university publishes the world's best-known list of "misused, overused and useless phrases and words" that have crept into the English language. Released each January 1, the Word Banishment List is compiled from thousands of submissions by tallying the most-nominated linguistic fingernails across the blackboard, such as the following from

- the movies — "show me the money"
- business — "outsource," "multi-tasking" and "phone tag"
- the military — "de-water" (meaning "to bail")
- TV talk shows — "you go, girl!"
- radio call-in shows — "thank you for taking my call" and "long-time listener, first-time caller"
- sports — "play one game at a time"
- adult cliches — "been there, done that"
- teen slang — "whatev-er-r-r"

MOST QUOTABLE QUOTES

In *Michigan in Quotes* (Friede Publications), author Tom Powers compiled more than 1,000 entertaining, informative "reflections, observations, witticism and outbursts, all about Michigan," including

"On the first day...the Lord created fudge. And on the second day, He created Northern Michigan so people could get to the fudge."

— *Michigan Living*, August 1979

A Calhoun County Sheriff's Department official, commenting on his county's record 1,368 deer-car accidents in 1991 exclaimed, "The deer in our county have absolutely no respect for law enforcement and frankly we're sick of it."

A Hastings resident in 1993, explaining why she thought her town had been listed as one of the "100 Best Small Towns in America" replied, "We're like Mayberry with an attitude."

MOST-PROLIFIC PIOUS PUBLISHER

ZONDERVAN PUBLISHING HOUSE. Grand Rapids.

This 67-year-old firm ranks among the world's largest publisher of religious books and materials. Its catalog features more than 2,000 titles by some 800 authors.

(616) 698-6900   www.zondervan.com

MOST FAITHFUL DRIVE-IN

WOODLAND DRIVE-IN CHURCH. Grand Rapids.

Each Sunday at 11 a.m. some 60 vehicles carrying members of a branch of the Fifth Reformed Church pull into parking spots at a former drive-in theater, where the worshippers then tune their car radios to a designated FM band and, without leaving their vehicles, listen to and watch their minister preach from the top of a 30-foot-high platform. The unique 30-year-old place of worship is reputed to be the only year-round drive-up church in the northeastern U. S.

(616) 942-5980

BEST PLACE TO ADMIRE NUNS' HABITS

DOLL MUSEUM. Indian River.

Filling glass cases in the basement below the gift shop at the world's largest crucifix (p. 84) are 525 dolls and 20 mannequins dressed in garb unique to 217 different religious orders, from Adorers of the Precious Blood (Canada) to the Xaverian Missionary Fathers and Brothers (Rome, Italy). Most all of the dolls in what is said to be the world's largest such collection are sisters in dress ranging from countless variations of traditional black-and-white floor-length habits to contemporary, comparatively colorful business suits.

(231) 238-8973

MOST-COMPELLING CROSS RITE BELOW THE SURFACE

CROSS IN THE BAY. Petoskey.

Lying on the bottom of Little Traverse Bay is a beautiful one-ton marble crucifix, a monument originally placed in 1962 as a memorial to divers that has also become a unique sanctuary. Submerged 24 feet and marked in the summer by a buoy, the life-size statue of Christ on the cross is regularly visited by boaters and divers, many of whom come to worship underwater.

And on one weekend each winter, conditions permitting, more than a thousand people follow a marked path 1,200 feet from shore to the frozen site. There they kneel down on the ice and, through large holes cut by local "keepers of the cross," take in unforgettable — many say inspirational — views of the chiseled sculpture, especially at night when its facets are illuminated by spotlights.

(800) 845-2828   (231) 347-4150

MOST-FAR-REACHING IMPACT OF THE "SAY YES TO MICHIGAN" CAMPAIGN

In 1983 a group of Oklahoma tourists paid thousands of dollars apiece for the chance to go to an area of China never before visited by an American. As their bus pulled up to the promised destination in remote Inner Mongolia, an excited high-ranking local official greeted the visitors by proudly flashing a *Say Yes to Michigan* button he had received from a Michigan State student who had bicycled through the area the week before.

MOST-CULTURED STATE PARK

INTERLOCHEN STATE PARK. Interlochen.

Most campers and day-use visitors here cross M-37 to tour the world-renowned Interlochen Center for the Arts and take in free daily plays, exhibitions and concerts.

(231) 276-9511

FINEST FREE JAZZ GIG

MONTREUX JAZZ FESTIVAL. Detroit.

Hart Plaza is the open-air venue for North America's largest free jazz festival, with more than 120 acts performing continuously on five stages from noon to 11 p.m. daily during four summer-ending days each year.

(313) 963-7622   www.montreuxdetroitjazz.com

MOST-EDUCATIONAL POW WOW

DANCE FOR MOTHER EARTH. Ann Arbor.

A pow wow is a social gathering where Native Americans share customs, cultures and traditions. And this celebration of the Earth's renewal, held annually and open to the public since 1972, is rated as one of North America's top opportunities to learn and experience Indian songs, dances, and arts and crafts. For one March weekend at Crisler Arena more than 1,000 of the continent's best Native American singers, dancers and drummers from several dozen tribes perform while every intricacy and nuance is explained to spectators.

MOST-SUCCESSFUL STATEWIDE PUBLIC LITTER-ACY PROGRAMS

ADOPT A HIGHWAY, ADOPT A FOREST, AND ADOPT A PARK.

Nearly 7,000 miles of Michigan roads, more than 100,000 acres of forest land, and some 25 state parks are cleaner and more beautiful due to several thousand volunteers who have worked since 1990 in these popular, ongoing public service projects. Under the the auspices and direction of state government agencies, groups of six or more people from schools, businesses, churches, scouts, and other clubs and organizations sign contracts to "adopt" small segments of Michigan and then care for them by regularly picking up trash and carrying out other improvement projects.

(888) 797-6272

MOST-DIRECT WAY TO MAKE POLITICAL HAY

To demonstrate his commitment to economy in state government, Governor John S. Barry during the 1840s had the grass that was cut on the capitol lawn baled and sold as hay.

MOST-CHARITABLE ONE-NIGHT AFFAIR

NORTH AMERICAN AUTO SHOW CHARITY PREVIEW. Detroit.

Detroit's largest black-tie party is unprecedented in three ways: 1) it's so popular that the $250 admission tickets not only sell out well in advance, but also are sometimes scalped for $1,000, 2) an unheard of 97 percent of the gate, about $4 million, goes directly to several children's charities, and 3) as a result, the event is believed to rank as the nation's largest one-night fund raiser.

Yet, on the surface at least, it's low key. For a few evening hours each January, 17,000 party-goers representing Detroit society and the international auto industry sip inexpensive champagne out of plastic cups while inspecting new-model vehicles and each other.

FIRST-DEGREE EXPOSURE

THE NAKED MILE. Ann Arbor.

Late each April several hundred University of Michigan seniors celebrate their last day of school by jogging naked through the campus, with a brief break on the Museum of Art's steps to sing "Hail to the Victors." The late-night streak also draws 8,000-10,000 cheering, camera-carrying spectators.

WILDEST ART EXPO

MICHIGAN WILDLIFE ART FESTIVAL.

The Midwest's largest wildlife art show, a three-day event produced each spring by the Michigan Wildlife Habitat Foundation, features works by nearly 60 painters, sculptors, carvers, photographers and other artists.

(517) 882-3630   www.mwhf.org

MOST-POPULAR, PRESTIGIOUS ART FAIR

ANN ARBOR ART FAIR. Ann Arbor.

More than a half million shoppers hand over an estimated $50 million to 1,000 exhibitors selling juried items ranging from expensive world-class gallery pieces to affordable, unique crafts at this four-day July three-fairs-in one event, the largest of its kind in the Midwest.

(734) 995-7281

FINEST FROZEN GALLERY

PLYMOUTH ICE SCULPTURING SPECTACULAR. Plymouth.

Artists — using chain saws, routers, drills, chisels, flat irons and other tools — transform 350 tons of ice into more than 200 glistening sculptures during North America's oldest and largest ice-carving gathering. Nearly a half million spectators, most carrying cameras, typically view the beautiful, sometimes huge and spectacular frozen creations, which are displayed throughout downtown Plymouth for six days each January.

(734) 459-9157   www.oeonline.com/plymouthice

BEST SAY-YES-TO-MICHIGAN-ARTISTS GALLERY

JOYCE PETTER GALLERY. Douglas/Saugatuck.

This popular resort/vacation area's largest gallery displays works of more Michigan artists than any other in the state, according to *Michigan Living* magazine.

(616) 857-7861   www.joycepettergallery.com

FINEST FINE-ARTS MUSEUM

DETROIT INSTITUTE OF ARTS. Detroit.

Housing a tremendous depth and breadth of great art, the huge DIA complex consistently ranks as one of the nation's top-six art museums. Sixty thousand paintings, sculptures and other exhibits include masterpieces and other important works by such well-known artists as Rembrandt, van Gogh, Renoir, Whistler, Picasso, Degas, and Matisse.

(313) 833-7900   www.dia.org

MOST-MOVING STATION-ARY ART

PEOPLE MOVER
ART IN THE STATIONS.
Detroit.

Two million dollars worth of publicly funded artwork decorates the 13 stations of the elevated passenger rail system that loops through the Motor City's downtown area. Eighteen large, beautiful works by 15 artists include a realistic statue of a man reading a newspaper, cast-bronze "hurrying commuters," (photo below), a free-form neon tube sculpture, a 90-foot-long porcelain panel composition, two bronze sculptures, and 12 colorful, varied mosaic tile murals.

(800) 541-7245

MOST-ON-TRACK ART EXHIBIT

MICHIGAN ARTRAIN.

Michigan's unique contribution to the national development of art appreciation is a traveling art museum set up in five railroad cars. Since 1971, changing, thematic, instructive exhibitions plus an artist's studio and museum shop set up in three converted passenger cars, a baggage car, and a caboose have toured throughout Michigan and 42 other states.

www.diamondbullet.com/Artrain/

MOST-ARTISTIC SALMON BYPASS

GRAND RIVER.
Grand Rapids.

Jutting out of the west bank of the Grand River across from downtown Grand Rapids is a large, angular concrete sculpture designed to provide salmon with an easy detour around the Sixth Street Dam. Instead of a single 14-foot jump into the face of that minifalls, the fish make successive 2-foot leaps up a series of seven ledges with underwater nooks and crannies that help keep them from backsliding.

For humans, this is walk-on art, with multileveled above-water platforms, stairs and walkways offering excellent views of the large fish, especially during fall migration from early September to late October.

MOST-CULTURAL TRAILS

MICHIGAN LEGACY ART PARK.
Thompsonville.

Two dozen pieces of large-scale art line a 2-mile-long hiking/cross-country ski trail that steeply rises and falls while looping through hardwoods at Crystal Mountain Resort. A 4-foot-long green metal frog, a small stockade-style labyrinth, the "Red Demon" sculpture, and several canted stacks of logs titled "Sawpaths" are among the varied works permanently displayed in the one-of-a-kind outdoor gallery.

P.O. Box 82, Harbor Springs MI 49740-0882

MOST-REMARKABLE HAND-CRAFTED RUSTIC FURNITURE

SHRINE OF THE PINES. Baldwin.

For more than 30 years beginning in 1920, Raymond W. "Bud" Overholzer painstakingly transformed white pine stumps, slabs, roots and other lumbering-era leftovers into an incredible collection of more than 200 functional, ergonomic, beautiful pieces of furniture, furnishings and utensils. Among the hunting and fishing guide's amazing creations, on display in a single-room rustic log cabin overlooking the Pere Marquette River, are a root rocking chair so perfectly balanced it moves 55 times with a single start and a dining table for 12 made from a 700-pound stump, with root legs hollowed out to store napkins and silverware.

(231) 745-7892

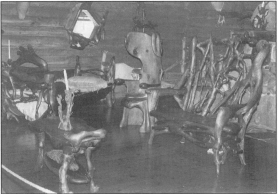

MOST-DIVERTING DINING DECOR

LEGS INN. Cross Village.

Gnarled roots, twisted limbs, sturdy stumps, driftwood, fieldstones, and other local "found" materials were used by Polish immigrant Stanislaw Smolak from 1921 to 1968 to construct, furnish and decorate this one-of-a-kind, out-of-the-way bar/restaurant.

The rustic building is a gallery of attention-grabbing creations. Fronting a huge stone fireplace, for instance, are heavily shellacked dining tables constructed of pine logs, split and fastened together flat-side up and supported by root legs. Two-person tables in the bar are composed of 3-foot-high curved sections of inch-thick bark topped with pine slabs. The bar itself is a huge log laid on its side and planed flat on top. And intricate, elaborate nature- and hand-carved driftwood sculptures cover walls and ceilings.

(616) 745-7892

SINGULAR STRUCTURES

FASTEST ICE-FISHING SHANTY

A one-of-a-kind wooden fishing shack attached to skis and powered by an airplane engine has transported its Escanaba builder/ owner from ice-angling coldspot to hotspot at speeds up to 100 mph since 1994.

MOST-ECCENTRIC EARLY RECYCLING EFFORT

JOHN J. MAKINEN HOUSE. Kaleva.

In 1941 the retired owner of a Manistee County bottling company built a 9-room home with outer walls constructed of 60,000 pop bottles laid on their sides in mortar, bottoms facing out and plastered over on the inside. The unusual material has proved durable; the structure currently serves as home to the Kaleva Historical Society.

MOST-COMICAL COTTAGE

TEENIE WEENIE PICKLE BARREL. Grand Marais.

This former summer home of artists William and Mary Donahey is a life-size replica of pickle-barrel dwellings used "under a rose bush in the woods" by their popular 1920s *Chicago Tribune* cartoon strip "Teenie Weenie" characters. The unique structure — a small staved-barrel foyer connected to a 2-story living-quarters barrel — today houses the area's tourist information center.

MOST-DELIGHTFUL GNOME HOMES

EARL YOUNG HOUSES. Charlevoix.

Nonarchitect Earl Young took local materials such as limestone, fieldstone, boulders and shipwreck timber and, for 30 years beginning in the mid-1920s, fashioned them into two dozen of the most-uniquely designed dwellings in Michigan. Lacking many straight lines, the small structures look like they naturally sprouted and grew from plots near Lake Michigan. Their smooth, irregular curves; unique, large fireplaces; cedar-shake roofs, and cottage size give the appearance of medieval residences for Snow White's Seven Dwarfs.

(231) 547-2101

MOST-LUXURIOUS RUSTIC GETAWAY

GRANOT LOMA. Marquette.

The phenomenal, deceptively primitive-looking main lodge that kisses Lake Superior at this isolated 10,000-acre private summer estate was created during the early 1920s largely from local, natural materials. Tons of stones hauled from local fields form the foundation that supports the mammoth L-shaped, three-story structure. Exterior walls are spruce logs hand-rubbed to match the color of dried pine needles, and slate slabs for the roof were custom-selected from area quarries to blend with the colors of surrounding trees. The 64,000 square-foot interior takes in 32 fireplaces and 50 rooms "wallpapered" with birch and cedar bark, arranged with hand-crafted wood furniture, and decorated with American Indian artifacts.

PLUSHEST PLAYHOUSES

MEADOW BROOK HALL. Rochester.

A few hundred yards away from the fabulous 100-room Tudor-style mansion built in 1929 for John Dodge's widow and her new husband is a proportionately fabulous 600-square-foot brick playhouse built for their daughter. The fully furnished six-room mini-mansion included the first all-electric kitchen in Michigan.

(248) 370-3140

FORD HOUSE. Grosse Pointe Shores.

A few hundred yards from a 60-room, 30,000-square-foot Cotswold-style mansion built in 1930 for Henry Ford's only son, Edsel, and his wife, Eleanor, is a similar-style Play House scaled down to fit a child 7-9 years old. A sitting room, for instance, comes with a small working fireplace, the bathroom includes child-size working fixtures, and the kitchen is equipped with a working sink and icebox. The elaborate building was a gift from Mrs. Henry Ford I to her only granddaughter, Josephine.

(313) 884-4222   www.fordhouse.org

GLITZIEST BACHELOR PAD

FISHER MANSION. Detroit.

During the Roaring Twenties, Lawrence Fisher — one of the founders of the Fisher Body Company and, later, president of Cadillac Motors — built a dazzling 52,000-square-foot mansion where he lived and playboyed for nearly 30 years until his first marriage at age 62.

From the outside, the home, which is open for tours, looks like a large, but plain Spanish hacienda.

Inside, however, style and decor of the 36 rooms is a flamboyant, colorful, eclectic mix — German castle, French chateau, Swiss chalet, Italian countryside, classic Japanese and art deco, for examples.

And champagne that spewed continuously from the mouth of a solid-silver head of Neptune plus a dusk-to-dawn changing image of the night sky projected onto the ballroom ceiling were two of many indulgences enjoyed by guests at lavish parties thrown here.

(313) 331-6740   www.fishermansion.org

MOST-ELABORATE VINTAGE SKYSCRAPERS

FISHER BUILDING. Detroit.

Since its completion in 1928, the 650,000 square-foot landmark Fisher Building has been called "Detroit's largest art object" and for good reason. Forty varieties of marble were imported from around the world to construct the tiered, Gothic 28-story "Golden Tower," whose exterior is trimmed in solid bronze.

The dominant feature of the elaborate interior is a cavernous 600-foot-long, 30-foot-wide, 3-story-high central arcade painted with mosaics, frescoes and other works by Hungarian artist Geza Maroti. Crystal chandeliers weighing from one to three tons hang from the arcade's hand-painted, gilded ceiling, and even the structure's smallest features, such as mailboxes, are artistically treated.

GUARDIAN BUILDING. Detroit.

"The Guardian Building is one of the most exuberant Art Deco skyscrapers built in America," says architectural historian Kathryn Bishop Eckert in *Buildings of Michigan* (Oxford University Press) and ranks with the Fisher Building, according to *Hunts' Highlights of Michigan* (Midwestern Guides), "as the most fantastic of Detroit's remarkable collection of 1920s office buildings."

Brilliantly colored Arts and Crafts tilework is the most-spectacular feature of this cathedral-like, double-towered former bank building, which covers an entire city block. Bands formed with green and white tiles, for instance, interrupt the orange-brick exterior; Pewabic and Rookwood tiles cover a half dome over the main entrance; and multicolored terra cotta and glazed tiles in geometric designs decorate the interior. Other outstanding visual effects include blood-red marble walls in the main lobby and a huge mural map of Michigan covering an entire wall of the former banking area.

MOST-BEAUTIFUL, RESTORED VICTORIAN MANSION

CHARLES H. HACKLEY HOUSE. Muskegon.

During the 1990s this neglected century-old, clapboard-sided, wood-frame mansion was painstakingly and completely restored to its original orgy of shape, texture and color. Twenty-eight different colors and shades matching the original paint cover gables, bays, towers, porches, latticework, spindles, posts and other ornate exterior features. Sixteen stained glass windows filter light onto lavish fabric-, stencil-, tile-, and metal-covered walls and intricately carved cherry, oak and butternut woodwork. Filled with period furnishings, including those of the original lumber-baron owner, Muskegon's most-famous house is "the finest restored Queen Anne house in North America,"says the Muskegon County Museum director in *Hunts' Highlights of Michigan* (Midwestern Guides).

(231) 722-7578

MOST A-PEALING BELFRIES

■ The state's best-known and the world's third-heaviest carillon — a 55-bell, 100-ton instrument — has rung out over the University of Michigan Ann Arbor campus from the top of 212-foot-high Burton Tower since 1936. During half-hour noon weekday concerts, students, faculty and visitors can climb to the top of the campus landmark and watch the carilloneur strike wooden keys connected to steel wires that pull clappers against the bronze cast bells.

(734) 764-2539

■ For an hour each summer Sunday afternoon, the world's second-largest carillon — 77 bronze bells weighing 66 tons — peals fugues and other music from the tower of the imposing Kirk in the Hills Presbyterian Church in Bloomfield Hills.

(248) 626-2515

MOST-REGAL MAIL DROP

(**Former**) POST OFFICE. Saginaw.

This massive century-old limestone structure is "...one of the fanciest post offices ever built in the country," says architectural historian Kathryn B. Eckert in *Buildings of Michigan* (Oxford University Press). The imposing chateau-like building — with round corner-towers, pointed peaks, carved finials, and steeply pitched red slate roof — is home to the Museum of Saginaw County History.

(517) 752-2861

MOST-DOMINEERING DOMES

SUPERIOR DOME. Northern Michigan University, Marquette.

This 150-foot-tall, 5-acre "inverted bowl" is the world's largest wooden sports dome. Constructed of crisscrossing Douglas fir beams and arches decked with more than 100 miles of tongue-and-groove planking, the $21 million structure opened in 1991 as a training center for prospective U.S. Olympic athletes.

Today the Yooper Dome, as it is also called, serves as home to NMU's football team and as a multipurpose recreational facility for students, faculty, and area citizens and visitors.

SILVERDOME. Pontiac.

The 10-acre translucent fiberglass roof of the Pontiac Silverdome is the largest in the world to be supported by air pressure only.

BIGGEST INDOOR BOAT

HANGING ARK. Canton.

A 165-foot-long, 48-foot-wide ark-shaped vessel suspended from the interior ceiling of the Yazaki North American Corp. office building is the largest non-floating vessel in the world. The beautiful mahogany 20-ton ship holds the electronics company's research and archival library.

BEST-LOOKING MASONRY

DETROIT MASONIC TEMPLE.

Ten- and 14-story medieval towers connected by a long, 7-story auditorium building make up "the largest and most beautiful Masonic temple in the world," says Kathryn Bishop Eckert in *Buildings of Michigan* (Oxford University Press). Completed in 1926, the huge, gray limestone structure comprises distinctly designed and decorated cathedrals, a drill hall, ballrooms, offices, guest rooms, billiard rooms and gymnasiums used by members of 47 fraternal orders. The intimate 4,600-seat auditorium, open to the public, is a favorite Detroit venue for performers and audiences.

MOST-BEAUTIFUL ROCK-SOLID FORMER FARM

STONE VILLAGE. Jackson.

Twelve uniquely beautiful towered and turreted dairy farm buildings — including a main house, a tenant house, a swine barn, a creamery, and a massive 18,000-square-foot barn — were constructed of cut fieldstone at the end of the 18th century by English stonemasons. The complex now operates as an art and theatrical center.

(517) 789-7913

MOST-IMPRESSIVE BARN RERAISING

THUMB OCTAGON BARN. Gagetown.

The largest and best-preserved of Michigan's few remaining octagon barns was built in 1923-24 and carefully restored in 1997 by Amish craftsmen and other volunteers using traditional skills, techniques, and "armstrong-," not electricity-powered, tools.

Each of the structure's eight sides rises 42 feet, and the shingled roof slopes up nearly another 30 feet to its peak. Three hundred window panes light 16,000 square feet of floor space that originally held hay.

(517) 665-0081

Friends of the Thumb Octagon Barn

LONGEST-LASTING COVERED BRIDGES

Only three original 19th-century wooden covered bridges remain in Michigan. The classic, historic, barn-like structures were so constructed to protect the bridge floor and underpinnings against the decaying effects of weather.

FALLASBURG. Lowell.

LANGLEY. Centreville.

WHITES. Smyrna.

Constructed of white pine latticework trusses, 4- by 10-inch floor beams, and 4- by 6-inch stringers in 1871 at a cost of $1,500, this 12-foot-high structure still carries vehicles 100 feet across the Flat River.

Michigan's longest extant covered bridge, a rare three-span timber structure, has stretched 282 feet across the backwater of the St. Joseph River to Sturgis Dam since 1887.

Constructed of hand-hewn trusses and rough pine boards held together with wooden pegs and hand-cut square iron nails, this beautiful 14-foot-wide bridge has carried traffic 116 feet across the Flat River since 1867.

BEST PLACE TO STARE AT STUMPS

TRUFANT.

Instead of burning thousands of large white pine stumps left by lumberman, Danish farmers in western Montcalm County ripped them from the ground, roots and all, and lined them along field edges. As these natural fences were replaced by more-modern versions, so many Trufant-area home and business owners hauled individual specimens — with intricately twisted root patterns beautifully weathered clean and gray — onto their property as adornments that the tiny town calls itself the Stump Fence Capital of the United States.

BIGGEST BAVARIAN BRIDGE

HOLZ-BRUCKE. Frankenmuth.

During the late 1970's what was reported to be the largest wooden covered bridge built in the 20th century was pieced together on land and, as was done in the 19th century, oxen were then used to place the 239-foot-long structure into position over the Cass River.

(517) 652-6106

LONGEST TREES TO TEES

GARLAND RESORT. Lewiston.

Golfers playing this four-star resort's signature Fountains course ride their carts over County Road 489 on the Midwest's longest single-span log bridge. Stretching some 80 feet between earthen approaches and stone support pillars, the 10-foot-wide, rustic-looking structure is constructed of log and steel bracing and a plank roadway protected by a cedar-shake roof.

(800) 968-0042

MOST-UNIQUE BRIDGINGS OF SMALL GAPS

SIPHON BRIDGE. Manistique.

Believe it or not, as Ripley would say and in this case did, the road surface of the 300-foot-long bridge that carries M-94 over the Manistique River in Manistique is well below water level. The river laps at the top of 4-foot-high concrete fences that edge the bridge, while atmospheric pressure forces the water under the near-century-old structure.

TRIDGE. Midland.

This unique — some say the only one of its kind in the world — pedestrian bridge connects three land areas separated by the confluence of the Chippewa and Tittabawassee rivers. From a hub built on a pier at the middle of the flows, walkways suspended from large, laminated wooden arches reach 100 yards in three different directions to land.

MOST-DRAMATIC LAND VIEWS OF THE MACKINAC BRIDGE

BOULEVARD DRIVE, OFF US-2 WEST OF ST. IGNACE.

Most observers say the perspectives that best reveal the architecture, art — some even say poetry — of Michigan's best-known landmark come from atop a high bluff at Father Marquette National Memorial and from a shore-hugging public parking area fronting the same bluff and only yards away from the mammoth structure's north approach.

MOST-INSPIRATIONAL VIEWS OF THE MACKINAC BRIDGE

The only public close-up views of the Mackinac Bridge from the water come during summer Vesper Cruises, low-key, ecumenical church services conducted aboard ferries that depart on Sunday evenings from Mackinaw City and Tuesday evenings from St. Ignace. Halfway through the 90-minute round trip, each ferry slowly weaves through and around the bridge's colossal concrete tower bases and cable anchorages.

Then at sunset, the engines shut off and passengers contemplate and reflect while their temporary chapel silently bobs under the enormous structure.

(800) 338-6660   (800) 666-0160

MOST ACCURATE LEADS TO LIGHTHOUSES

A TRAVELER'S GUIDE TO 116 MICHIGAN LIGHTHOUSES
(Friede Publications) by the Penrose family.

This excellent guidebook is a must for those who want to experience Michigan's colorful, historic lighthouses up-close and personal. Concise text combines colorful description, fascinating history and practical advice, and beautiful black-and-white photographs show what to expect. And most important, accurate maps and directions lead the way *to* the silent sentinels.

MOST-DISTINCT LIGHTHOUSE

WILLIAM H. LIVINGSTONE MEMORIAL LIGHT. Detroit.
This historic structure, a fluted column that rises 65 feet from the west end of Belle Isle, is the only lighthouse in the nation constructed of marble.

Penrose Outdoor Photography

MOST-DISTINCTIVE LIGHTHOUSE PAINT JOB

Penrose Outdoor Photography

WHITE SHOAL LIGHT. Lake Michigan.
The cylindrical tower of this otherwise plain off-shore light 20 miles west of the Mackinac Bridge has been painted with red and white spirals that wind up the structure as on a barber pole.

MOST-MODERN PLACE TO GET STARRY-EYED

DELTA COLLEGE PLANETARIUM
SCIENCE LEARNING CENTER. Bay City.
This $8.75 million NASA-funded facility opened in 1996 as Michigan's most high-tech place to experience astral projections. Computerized state-of-the-art projection and special-effects equipment is used to depict the night sky — stars, planets, moons, comets, asteroids, nebulae and other heavenly phenomena — on a 50-foot-diameter glass dome. Visitors are then treated to a variety of cosmic perspectives from vantage points throughout the universe as well as time.
(517) 667-2260

MOST-UNIQUELY DESIGNED WATER TOWERS

KALAMAZOO REGIONAL PSYCHIATRIC HOSPITAL.

This 175-foot-high water-tank enclosure, built in 1895, resembles the tower of a medieval castle.

FRIENDLIEST WATER TOWER

WEST BRANCH.
A familiar, black-on-yellow "smiley face" has grinned down at I-75 travelers from one of West Branch's two water towers since 1974.

MANISTIQUE.

Eight red-brick walls, each with an arch window near the top, rise from a substantial concrete and brick base to a red metal dome. The distinctive 200-foot-high structure has provided water to Manistique residents since 1922.

YPSILANTI.

This giant stone-clad, century-old toadstool sprouts up 170 feet from the highest point in the region, at the edge of Eastern Michigan University.

MOST CREATIVELY CONCRETE JURASSIC PARK

DINOSAUR GARDENS PREHISTORIC ZOO. Ossineke.
Set along a trail that winds through a lush, prehistoric-looking 40-acre cedar swamp are more than two dozen life-size, realistic (except for recent bright-colored paint jobs) reproductions of dinosaurs, including an 80-foot-high, 160,000-pound Brontosaurus. The in-

triguing sculptures were created from 1935 to 1967 by a local artist who, using no power tools, fashioned wire skeletons and painstakingly fleshed them out with a mixture of concrete, gravel and deer hair.

(517) 471-5477

GREATEST CONTRIVED COLOSSUSES

TIRE. Allen Park.

A 1964-65 World's Fair ferris wheel was covered with fiberglass and transformed into a 9-story-high, 10-ton replica of a Uniroyal wheel and tire that stands upright only yards off eastbound I-94.

World's Largest Tire, circa 1995. In 1998 the wheel was given a more modern look plus fitted with a 10-foot silvery nail in its tread to demonstrate a Uniroyal product that keeps rolling when punctured.

HIAWATHA. Ironwood.

A 52-foot-tall, 9-ton fiberglass statue of Hiawatha — called the world's largest Indian — stands watch over Michigan's westernmost city.

TROUT. Kalkaska.

A 17-foot-long brook trout has appeared rigor mortised in midleap from a small fountain since 1966. The steel-reinforced fiberglass sculpture was erected as a memorial to the state's official fish and as a draw to Kalkaska's National Trout Festival.

STOVE. Detroit.

This 3-story-high replica of a late-19th-century cooking/heating appliance was originally erected in 1893 as a symbol of Detroit's dominance of the stove industry at the time.

Constructed of a metal frame covered with oak carved and painted to look like cast iron, the Detroit landmark stood for nearly 80 years before being dismantled but not discarded. In 1998 volunteers painstakingly restored and reassembled the 15-ton "Garland" model on the Michigan State Fairgrounds.

WEATHERVANE. Montague.

The 26-foot-long black arrow of a 48-foot-tall aluminum weathervane topped with a 14-foot-long replica of a Great lakes lumbering era schooner has told Montague and Whitehall residents which way the wind is blowing since 1984.

MOST-MONUMENTAL MONUMENTS

Except for buildings, Michigan is relatively free of large or ostentatious memorials to important, influential, and famous sports, government, education, military, business and other figures who have come from the state.

Three that standout are

SHRINE OF THE SNOWSHOE PRIEST. L'Anse.

Five laminated wood beams arch up from concrete tepees to meet at a central stainless-steel cloud that supports a 35-foot-tall statue of Father Frederick Baraga clutching a 7-foot-high cross and a pair of 26-foot-long snowshoes. To teach, advise and minister to area Indians during the winters a century and a half ago, Fr. Baraga snowshoed great distances over the rugged U.P. terrain.

(906) 524-7444

CROSS IN THE WOODS. Indian River.

What is said to be the world's largest crucifix began as a shrine to Kateri Tekakwitha, a Christian convert who, because of her devoted ministry to her fellow Native Americans, was made a Blessed by Pope John II in 1980. Completed in 1959, the Marshall Fredericks-designed sculpture is composed of a 7-ton bronze likeness of Christ attached to a 55-foot-tall, 22-foot-wide cross carved out of a single California redwood.

(616) 238-8973

JOE LOUIS FIST. Detroit.

A 4-ton, 24-foot-long bronze sculpture of the arm and fist of the world's longest-reigning, some say greatest-ever heavyweight boxing champion, is suspended from a quadrapod at the foot of Woodward Avenue in his home town.

MOST-INTERESTING OBSCURE MONUMENTS

HUGH GRAY CAIRN. Kewadin.

This out-of-the-way, pyramidal-shaped monument to the first secretary of the Michigan Tourism Association was constructed on the 45th parallel in 1938 from one rock from each of Michigan's 83 counties. Each stone is engraved with its county-of-origin name, and all pretty much look the same except for a small, round grindstone from Huron County; copper- and iron-containing specimens from Houghton and Iron counties, respectively; and a polished tombstone-looking rectangular piece of granite from Kent County.

GIPP MEMORIAL. Laurium.

A modest bronze plaque attached to a 15-foot-high Lake-Superior-stone pillar memorializes Laurium native George Gipp who, as a halfback coached by the legendary Knute Rockne, became Notre Dame's first All-American football player. During his senior season in 1920, Gipp contracted pneumonia and, while dying, uttered to Rockne the inspirational sports mantra, "win one for the Gipper."

HIGH ROCK BAY. Copper Harbor.

During the winter months in the 1960s and early '70s, small NASA rockets were blasted into space from this then-isolated area only yards from the Lake Superior shoreline. A plaque near the remains of a concrete-slab launch pad explains that the missiles were fired not as part of Cold War defense testing, but to gather weather data.

INITIAL POINT.

A monument on the Ingham County-Jackson County boundary east of US-127 marks the point from which all land surveying in Michigan has been done since 1812. The rock that was placed there by Michigan's first surveyors is on display at the Michigan Museum of Surveying (p. 94).

BATTLE OF MANILA CANNON. Three Oaks.

Three Oaks won this war trophy — captured by Admiral George Dewey during the Spanish-American War — by raising the largest per-capita contribution of any U.S. community for a memorial to the men of the *Maine*, sunk in Havana Harbor in 1898.

RECORD RELOCATIONS

DEZWANN. 1964.

This 240-year-old, 12-story windmill was disassembled in the Netherlands then shipped to Holland, Michigan. There amidst dikes and canals in a 36-acre park, its 66 tons of fir beams, cedar planking, orange brick, cedar-shake roof, gears and huge grinding stones were reassembled into the only authentic working windmill in America.

(616) 355-1030

GEM THEATRE. DETROIT. 1997.

To help make room for the construction of new professional athletic stadiums, this historic 5.5-million-pound brick structure was hydraulically jacked up 10 feet, placed on steel beams supported by 72 dollies fitted with 576 pneumatic tires, and then moved five blocks. The $1.5-million relocation gained an entry in the *Guinness Book of Records* (Guinness Media Inc.) as the heaviest building ever moved on rubber tires.

JENNINGS. 1921.

Mammoth trailer trucks moved this entire town — 100 homes and a sawmill — to Cadillac, 11 miles to the south. The tiny village had decided to relocate closer to the mill's potential customers, and specially built trucks accomplished the task at the rate of two houses every three days.

LARGEST LIMESTONE QUARRY

From a viewing platform off Business Route US-23 just south of Rogers City you can look over and down into a 5,000-acre, up-to-250-foot-deep canyon continually enlarged by the excavation of nearly pure limestone. Nearly ¾-billion tons of the sedimentary rock has been blasted and removed since 1912, leaving the world's biggest hole-of-its-kind in the ground.

MOST-SPECTACULAR DEMOLITION

J.L. HUDSON BUILDING. Detroit.

October 24, 1998. The 25-story red-brick landmark that had stood in downtown Detroit for nearly a century was reduced to a 33,000-ton mountain of rubble in just 30 explosively charged seconds. The spectacular, graceful demolition — a controlled free fall choreographed by 2,728 pounds of 1,200 hand-made, strategically placed, sequentially fired charges — set world records for both the tallest and largest steel buildings ever imploded.

RECORD RECONSTRUCTION

A St. Joseph man entered the *Guinness Book of World Records* (Guinness Media, Inc.) in 1999 for having had the most body joints surgically replaced. Because of severe rheumatoid arthritis, the retiree had had all 12 major joints — both shoulders, both elbows, both wrists, both hips, both knees and both ankles — replaced, some twice, over a period of 16 years.

LIVING IN THE PAST

BIG MISTAKES
THAT TURNED OUT TO BE BIGGER BESTS

A FLAKY MOVE. Battle Creek, 1894.

While conducting experiments to invent a digestible substitute for bread, Will K. Kellogg absent-mindedly left a batch of boiled wheat to stand. Kellogg tried to reboil and compress the mixture, but a thin layer stuck to the rollers of his processing machines. As Kellogg removed the hardened mess with a knife, it fell in small pieces, and flake cereal had just been invented.

DRIVEN TO DISTRACTION. Detroit, 1896.

As Henry Ford prepared to test drive his first gasoline-powered "quadricycle," he discovered that he had built the contraption too wide to fit through his storage shed's door. So he smashed out part of a brick wall with a sledgehammer, took the vehicle on a successful trial run, and 30 years later fomented an industrial and lifestyle revolution

LIVELIEST PLACE TO RELIVE THE CIVIL WAR

CIVIL WAR MUSTER. Jackson.

More than a thousand Union and Confederate soldiers from around the country come to Cascade Falls Park each August for a weekend-long re-enactment of life during the Civil War. The largest gathering of its kind in the Midwest is a unique opportunity for spectators to step back in time as they walk through camps and battlefield hospitals and watch formations, drills, skirmishes and artillery and cavalry demonstrations. Highlight of the muster is a full-blown re-enactment of a major Civil War battle.
(517) 788-4320

RAREST VINTAGE-CAR MEET

OLD CAR FESTIVAL. Dearborn.

At the only gathering of its kind in the world, owners of 1890s through 1932 vehicles sometimes get tied up in 21st century-type traffic jams as they show off their vintage machines while driving over Greenfield Village's dirt and brick streets. During the unique two-day meet each June, drivers also demonstrate early motoring skills such as crank starting and getting a family of six into a car with only one door. And during a narrated pass-in-review, the more than 500 steam-, electric- and gasoline-powered vehicles move by in historical order.

(800) 835-5237

MOST-INTRIGUING PLACE TO WALK AMONG THE DEAD

ELMWOOD CEMETERY. Detroit.

The 52,000 tombstones spread over 86 rolling, beautifully landscaped acres here read like a *Who's Who* of Michigan's past. Opened in 1846, the state's most-historic, beautiful cemetery is the final resting place for seven Michigan governors, including 1848 presidential candidate Lewis Cass; 11 U.S. senators; 12 presidential cabinet members; 29 Detroit mayors including the most-recent to die, Coleman Young; 205 Civil War officers and men; explorers such as legendary surveyor-geologist Douglass Houghton; as well as important, influential captains of industry, publishers, artists, inventors, and other recognizables, such as Bernhard Stroh and James Vernor, both of whom began brewing their beverages in Detroit about a century and a half ago.

A map and brochures are available to help navigate paths that wind under mature sycamores, maples and oak.

(313) 567-3453

LONGEST-TERM COUNTY POLITICAL OFFICES

HISTORIC COURTHOUSE SQUARE. Berrien Springs.

Michigan's oldest, most-complete, extant complex of county government buildings includes an 1839 courthouse, a Victorian 2-story brick sheriff's house, an 1830s log cabin built for the county's first lawyer, and a blacksmith's forge.

(616) 471-1202

MOST-SCENIC RESTORED GHOST TOWN

FAYETTE.

"Fayette...is *the* most picturesque village, deserted or inhabited, in Michigan," writes Tom Powers in *Michigan State and National Parks: A Complete Guide* (Friede Publications).

Spectacularly set amidst towering limestone cliffs, white sand beaches and lush hardwood forests on the Garden Peninsula are more than 20 carefully restored buildings that made up a once-thriving pig-iron-processing company town. Now under the protection of the state-park system, the weathered-gray 130-year-old frame structures — including homes, an opera house, a hotel, a doctor's office and shops — plus squat stone kilns and tall limestone smokestacks overlook Big Bay de Noc's picturesque Snail Shell Harbor as they did more than a century ago.

(906) 644-2603

WILDEST CENTENNIAL CELEBRATION

To help celebrate the nation's 100th birthday, a 6-foot, 2-inch, 225-pound, tobacco-chewing madam named "Big Delia" and her employees built a huge pavilion at Muskegon, hired two bands, brought in hundreds of barrels of beer, invited their "sisters" from Chicago and Milwaukee, and threw a free July 4, 1876 party for more than a thousand area lumberjacks.

HIGHEST CONCENTRATIONS OF BEST-PRESERVED HISTORIC HOMES

HERITAGE HILL. Grand Rapids.

"(This) historic neighborhood of superbly detailed homes is probably the richest and most varied in the U.S.," says *Hunts' Highlights of Michigan* (Midwestern Guides). The 6-block-wide, 1½-mile long historic district just east of downtown Grand Rapids takes in hundreds of houses that reflect an architectural encyclopedia of more than 60 styles including Prairie, Chateauesque, Arts and Crafts, English Manor, Italianate, and Greek, Gothic, and Spanish Revival.

(616) 459-8950

MARSHALL.

Michigan's finest collection of preserved, restored historic homes, churches, public buildings and businesses makes up the country's largest National Historic Landmark District, small-urban category. A brochure-guided walking tour over the tree-lined streets features 136 of the more than 800 vintage structures, including an inordinate number of excellent examples of Italianate, Queen Anne, and Greek and Gothic Revival architecture from the 1840s and 1850s. And during the Annual Marshall Historic Home Tour held each September, thousands of visitors get intimate inside looks at a dozen or so of the most unique and elaborate mansions.

(800) 877-5163   www.historicmarshall.com

BAY VIEW.

Begun by Michigan Methodists in 1875 as a religious, Chautauqua-type tent encampment, the Bay View Association today comprises more than 400 gabled, turreted, dormered, pillared, porched, clapboard-sided and gingerbread-trimmed Victorian cottages so beautifully and accurately maintained that the entire village is on the National Register of Historic Places. Most of the elaborate summer homes plus 30 uniquely beautiful common-use buildings were constructed before 1900 on 338 acres of tree-lined, winding streets that follow a series of natural terraces overlooking Little Traverse Bay.

(800) 845-2828   www.boynecountry.com

MOST-REALISTICALLY RESTORED FORTS

COLONIAL MICHILIMACKINAC. Mackinaw City.

Forty years of painstaking work at Michigan's second state park and the country's oldest ongoing archaeological site has resulted in a reconstruction so authentic that it has earned National Historic Landmark designation. Abandoned and burned more than two centuries ago, this wood-stockaded trading village/military outpost has been accurately reproduced to look exactly as it did in the 1770s based on the exposing of original foundations, the excavation of millions of artifacts, and careful analysis of an abundance of written accounts of life here.

(231) 436-5563

FORT MACKINAC. Mackinac Island.

This state-park historic site includes some of Michigan's oldest structures, some dating to the 1780s. Perched on a high bluff overlooking Mackinac Island's fudge and gift shops, the complex comprises 14 restored, original buildings including barracks, officers quarters, blockhouses, a canteen and a post commissary, most protected by a surrounding wall of white limestone thick enough to withstand cannon fire.

(231) 436-5563

FORT WILKINS. Copper Harbor.

To preserve law and order during Michigan's copper mining boom this fort was constructed in 1844 on a thin strip of forestland that separates Lake Fanny Hooe from Lake Superior. During only five years of use, it underwent little change and so "is one of the few classic examples of the wood forts that sprouted up along the American frontier during the mid-1800s," writes Tom Powers in *Michigan State and National Parks: A Complete Guide* (Friede Publications).

Inside a reconstructed log palisade are 19 meticulously restored and authentically furnished buildings — most constructed of hewn timber on stone foundations — including officers quarters, mess hall, company barracks, a bakery, a hospital, a sutlers building, a powder magazine, and an ice house.

(906) 289-4215

BEST HISTORIC-BUILDING COLLECTION

GREENFIELD VILLAGE. Dearborn.

The nearly 100 homes, farms, stores, workshops and other buildings that make up this world-famous outdoor museum comprise three centuries' worth of landmarks, famous and mundane, that were plucked by Henry Ford from locations across the country, restored and then plunked down in his back yard in fascinating, unexpected juxtaposition. The Menlo Park, New Jersey, laboratory where Thomas Edison invented the incandescent lightbulb, for instance, is half a block from the Dayton, Ohio, shop where the Wright brothers built their first airplane; which is around the corner from the Detroit shed in which Henry Ford assembled his first automobile; which is down the street from the Logan County, Illinois, courthouse where Abraham Lincoln first practiced law.

(800) 835-5237   www.hfmgv.org

MOST-UNUSUAL EXHIBITS

■ When auto pioneer Henry Ford learned that his dear friend Thomas Edison was dying, he asked the famous inventor's son, Charles, to collect one of his father's last exhaled breaths. Charles and the attending physician did so, and the corked, sealed-in-paraffin vial is on display at the Henry Ford Museum in Dearborn.

■ Occasionally on display at Michigan State University's Anthony Hall is what is said to be the world's largest hairball ever expelled by or removed from a cow.

OVAL-OFFICE STANDOUT

GERALD R. FORD MUSEUM. Grand Rapids.

The political and personal life of the only U.S. president to come from Michigan is chronicled by high-tech multimedia, interactive exhibits that include a holographic guided tour of 11 White House rooms, a full-size replica of the Oval Office, and multi-screen video and light shows with surround-sound.

(616) 451-9263   www.lbjlib.utexas.edu/ford/

BEST NATURAL SCIENCE & HISTORY MUSEUM

EXHIBIT MUSEUM. University of Michigan, Ann Arbor.

"Not many other natural science museums in the country match the rarity and breadth of items on display here," says the authoritative *Hunts' Highlights of Michigan* (Midwestern Guides). Four floors of galleries are neatly crammed with dioramas, dinosaur fossils (p. 93), the Midwest's most-complete pterodactyl display (p. 95), an amazing mounted Michigan wildlife collection, a planetarium, and other exhibits and displays that explore anthropology, Native American cultures, Michigan wildlife, astronomy, biology, ecology, geology, mineralogy and other disciplines from prehistory to the present.

(734) 764-0478   www.exhibits.lsa.umich.edu

MOST-TELLING MASTODON TRACKS

EXHIBIT MUSEUM. University of Michigan, Ann Arbor.

As a 6-ton male mastodon slogged through the shallow water of a prehistoric Michigan lake, it left 20-inch-wide footprints in the firm sand bed. There they fossilized and lay hidden for 10,000 years until uncovered in 1992 during excavation of a pond near Saline. The 20 preserved tracks — so clear that paleontologist could tell exactly where the mammoth animal tripped over a log — are the largest, most-complete mastodon trackway ever found anywhere in the world.

(734) 764-0478   www.exhibits.lsa.umich.edu

BEST COLLECTIONS OF...

... AMERICAN THROWAWAYS

HENRY FORD MUSEUM. Dearborn.

The world's largest, most-fascinating private collection of Americana — a staggering number of artifacts salvaged from the nation's garages, attics, workshops, barns, offices, factories and streets since the Revolutionary War — is neatly crammed into a cavernous, 12-acre single-story complex fronted by an exact replica of Philadelphia's Independence Hall. Intermixed with impressive full-scale Smithsonian-type exhibits, the 220-year sampling of American refuse is organized by subject into more than 50 separate collections, many of which — lighting fixtures, tractors and timepieces, to name a few — are the country's or world's best.

(800) 835-5237 www.hfmgv.org

...BB GUNS

PLYMOUTH HISTORICAL MUSEUM. Plymouth.

For nearly 70 years beginning in 1890, Daisy BB guns were manufactured exclusively in Plymouth, earning the small town the reputation as the "air rifle capital of the world." Today, one room of the local-history museum is devoted to Daisy products, including a collection of the earliest models and the advertising that made young boys covet them.

(734) 455-8940

...CLASSIC CARS

GILMORE CLASSIC CAR CLUB OF AMERICA MUSEUM. Hickory Corners.

More than 150 vintage automobiles in showroom shape are displayed in eight large, red restored barns plus a replica 1930s service station. Included are a 1948 Tucker, a 1929 Duesenberg, a 1927 Bugattie Grand Sport Roadster, 15 Rolls Royces, and the world's largest collection of mint-condition Packards (20).

(616) 671-5089 www.gilmorecarmuseum.org

...DINOSAUR SKELETONS

EXHIBIT MUSEUM. University of Michigan, Ann Arbor.

The fossilized remains of seven dinosaurs — including the complete skeleton of a monstrous flesh-eating allosaurus — is the largest and best display of the extinct prehistoric giants available in Michigan.

(734) 764-0478 www.exhibits.lsa.umich.edu

...FLYABLE WORLD WAR II AIRCRAFT

KALAMAZOO AVIATION HISTORY MUSEUM. Kalamazoo.

More than 35 authentically and fully restored WWII aircraft are on display inside a mammoth 80,000-square-foot hangar complex. Half of the colorful craft are airworthy, including the reasons for the museum's nickname, "Air Zoo"— a Flying Tiger, an Aircobra, a Warhawk, and the world's only flyable collection of "cats," Wildcat, Hellcat, Tigercat and Bearcat.

(616) 382-6555

...ICE-HARVESTING PARAPHERNALIA

KNOWLTON'S ICE MUSEUM. Port Huron.

This unique museum holds the country's largest collection of tools, equipment and artifacts used in pre-electric appliance days to cut chunks of ice out of frozen rivers and lakes, insulate them in "cold houses,"and then deliver them to home and business ice-box refrigerators during warm weather.

(810) 987-7100

...MUSICAL INSTRUMENTS

STEARNS COLLECTION OF MUSICAL INSTRUMENTS. University of Michigan North Campus, Ann Arbor.

This comprehensive collection of rare, common, unique, old and new instruments from around the world numbers 2,200 (and growing). It includes, for just a few examples, a Tibetan drum made from a human skull, a Baroque cello, the first commercial Moog synthesizer, a pocket-size English signal horn, and shaped animal bones played like spoons.

(734) 763-4389

...OLD ORGANS

LEE CONKLIN ANTIQUE ORGAN MUSEUM. Hanover.

Seventy-six playable parlor, chapel and other antique pump-type reed organs, some from Civil War times, are on display and occasionally used to put on group miniconcerts.

(517) 563-2311

BEST PLACE TO...

...ABSORB JAZZ HISTORY

GRAYSTONE INTERNATIONAL JAZZ MUSEUM. Detroit.

The country's only public jazz museum comprises several rooms filled with music, videos, posters, album covers, instruments and other memorabilia chronologically arranged as an enthusiastic history of jazz and jazz greats such as Miles Davis, John Coltrane, Duke Ellington and Betty Carter.

(313) 963-3813

...CHECK OUT CUSTER'S FIRST THROUGH LAST STANDS

MONROE COUNTY HISTORICAL MUSEUM. Monroe.

Monroe's most-famous resident is George Armstrong Custer, who grew up in the city, married a local woman, and returned to the area often even after he had become a famous brigadier general. Not surprisingly then, the county historical museum houses the country's largest collection of Custer items, including his baby dress, swords, rifles, West Point cadet uniform, buffalo-hide robe, and elaborate buckskin suit adorned with beadwork and porcupine quills.

(734) 243-7137

...CRUNCH CELERY TIDBITS

CELERY FLATS INTERPRETIVE CENTER. Portage.

Tools, a demonstration greenhouse, planting beds, photos and other entertaining exhibits tell the story of how, from the 1890s to the 1930s, Dutch immigrants turned Kalamazoo area wetlands into one of the world's best-known and productive celery-growing regions.

(616) 329-4518

...FEEL LIKE A ROCKET MAN

MICHIGAN SPACE CENTER. Jackson.

Inside this 12,000-square-foot geodesic dome you get close-up looks at $40 million and 40 years worth of space-program hardware and artifacts, including the Apollo 9 Command Module, packets of space food, a moon rock, a mission-control console, a space-shuttle shower, unmanned satellites, and a wardrobe of space suits.

(517) 787-4425

...GET YOUR BEARINGS

MICHIGAN MUSEUM OF SURVEYING. Lansing.

During the early 1800s, surveyors in Michigan forded streams, slogged through swamps, and fended off wild animals to determine land boundaries for settlement. Today they ford streams, slog through swamps, and dodge traffic to legally describe property to prevent ownership disputes.

The techniques, tools and instruments they have used to section off the state are displayed in the country's only museum dedicated to the surveying profession. Emphasis is on hardware — hundreds of pieces, several more than a century-and-a-half-old — including brass sextants, sundials, protractors, levels, transits, and compasses plus a few state-of-the-art, digitalized, plastic-encased Global Positioning (satellite) System instruments.

(517) 484-6605

...LEARN THE ABCs OF THE CCC

CIVILIAN CONSERVATION CORP MUSEUM. Roscommon.

This one-of-a-kind museum, located in North Higgins Lake State Park, is dedicated to the more than 100,000 young unemployed Michigan men who, for $30 a month during the Great Depression, planted nearly 500 millions trees, stocked rivers and lakes with fish, and constructed dams, bridges, landing strips, roads, buildings, campgrounds and hiking trails. Exhibit buildings include a replica CCC barracks, an original "cone barn," and Michigan's first iron fire tower.

(517) 821-6125

...LISTEN TO OLD MUSIC-MAKERS

MUSIC HOUSE. Acme.

An incredible number and variety of self-playing instruments — from familiar tinny player pianos to a monstrous Belgian creation that reproduces the sounds of an entire dance orchestra — put on audio and visual shows inside a beautifully redone dairy farm haybarn and granary. Rich, clear miniconcerts by the antique, often-rare automated music machines reproduce the sounds that filled theaters, ballrooms, saloons and parlors around the world from the 1870s through the 1920s.

(231) 938-9300   www.musichouse.org

BEST PLACE TO...

...MUSE THE MOTOWN SOUND

MOTOWN MUSEUM. Detroit.

Mementoes and memorabilia from Michigan's most-phenomenal contribution to the music world are preserved in two small adjacent houses where Motown founder Berry Gordy launched his legendary entertainment empire. Several rooms inside Hitsville USA, as Gordy confidently and correctly labeled his humble living quarters/office/studio, are filled with instruments, costumes, photos, posters, album jackets, gold records and letters, all of which chronicle how Gordy took hundreds of talented black musicians and transformed them into world-famous stars.

Startling highlight for most visitors is small, crude Studio A, where hit after chart-busting hit was recorded.

(313) 875-2266

...PEER AT PTERODACTYLS

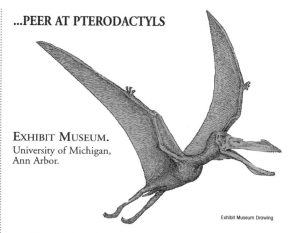

EXHIBIT MUSEUM. University of Michigan, Ann Arbor.

Exhibit Museum Drawing

The Midwest's most-comprehensive exhibit of 200-million-year-old "flying lizards" includes a full-size reconstruction, a skeleton model and fossil casts.

(734) 764-0478   www.exhibits.lsa.umich.edu

...PONDER PETROGLYPHS

SANILAC HISTORIC SITE. New Greenleaf.

The only known set of prehistoric Indian carvings in Michigan are open to public viewing at this out-of-the-way state park. There, along the banks of the Cass River some 400 to 1,100 years ago, ancient artists used stones, bones and antlers to laboriously carve and scratch more than 100 intriguing figures — birds, animals, humans, tracks and abstract patterns — into soft sandstone outcroppings.

(517) 242-2742

BEST PLACE TO...

...REALIZE THE HOLOCAUST

HOLOCAUST MEMORIAL CENTER. West Bloomfield.

Explicit displays, dioramas, films, photos and videotaped recollections of survivors grimly and emotionally re-create the horror surrounding the near extermination of European Jews by Adolph Hitler's Nazis carrying out their "Final Solution" during World War II.

(810) 661-0840   www.holocaustcenter.org

...RELIVE THE THE MACKINAC BRIDGE CONSTRUCTION

MACKINAC BRIDGE MUSEUM. Mackinaw City.

An informal but well-done collection of original equipment and tools — such as 6-foot-long wrenches, a spinning wheel that helped wind 42,000 miles of thin wire into 2-foot-thick cables, 60-pound ironworkers' tool belts, and a diving suit — plus other artifacts, photos and a continuous-play video combine to provide an excellent condensed replay of Michigan's most-dramatic construction project, completed in 1957.

(231) 436-5534

...SALUTE MICHIGAN VETERANS

MICHIGAN'S OWN MILITARY MUSEUM. Frankenmuth.

More than 300 meticulous displays honor the sacrifices and accomplishments of Michigan military men and women (plus ten astronauts) during war, conflict and peacetime. Included among the many artifacts, weapons, uniforms and memorabilia is the largest display of Congressional Medals of Honor (15) anywhere.

(517) 652-8005

...TIME WARP INTO A 19TH-CENTURY OFFICE

IXL OFFICE MUSEUM. Hermansville.

This elaborate three-story headquarters of a formerly prominent hardwood floor manufacturer stands intact, complete with original furnishings and equipment, as when used from 1883 through the 1920s. Huge oak rolltop desks, old Burroughs adding machines, inkwells, a mechanical clock, crank telephones, dictaphones, early versions of mimeograph machines (including original instructions), typewriters and ledgers all stand work-ready in the exceptionally well-preserved building.

(906) 498-2498   (906) 498-7724

...TRACK THE HISTORY OF SKIING

NATIONAL SKI HALL OF FAME AND MUSEUM. Ishpeming.

Displays of skis, poles and other equipment plus artifacts, photos and drawings trace the development of skiing from survival to sport — from prehistoric Scandinavian hunters who used crude slats to move within spear range of quarry to contemporary resort skiers gliding over machine-made snow.

(906) 485-6323   www.skihall.com

BEST PLACE TO TRACE MICHIGAN'S PAST

MICHIGAN HISTORICAL MUSEUM. Lansing.

Three hundred thousand-plus square feet of display space layered up five levels is divided into 27 galleries holding hundreds of exhibits that offer multi-faceted views of Michigan from prehistory to 1975. A life-size replica of a U.P. copper mine tunnel, a two-story lumber baron's mansion, and a one-room schoolhouse are among major displays that help illustrate Michigan's geological, political, social, cultural, agricultural and industrial past.

(517) 373-3559   www.sos.state.mi.us/history/history.html

MOST-COMPREHENSIVE, AUTHORITATIVE GENERAL MICHIGAN HISTORY BOOK

MICHIGAN: A HISTORY OF THE WOLVERINE STATE
(Wm. B. Eerdmans Publishing Co.) by Willis F. Dunbar, revised by George S. May

INDEX

WORLD'S

air-rifle capital 93

BEST
  chimpanzee exhibit 59

HIGHEST
  manmade ski jump 29

LARGEST
  air-supported roof 78
  and oldest resort hotel 25
  apple 58
  beaver pond 60
  bedding plant market 11
  breakfast 21
  cedar 56
  collection of dolls dressed in religious garb 69
  collection of mint-condition Packards 93
  concentration of auto showrooms 11
  cow hairball 92
  crucifix 84
  display of Congressional Medals of Honor 96
  freshwater boardwalk 49
  Great Lakes maritime museum 48
  Indian 83
  kohlrabi 58
  limestone quarry 86
  manufacturer of magic equipment 12
  most-complete mastodon trackway 92
  nonfloating vessel 78
  pasty bake 21
  pie 21
  polar bear exhibit 59
  private collection of Americana 93
  selection of exotic skin shoes 13
  single-day car cruise 8
  stand of bird's-eye maple 56
  submarine sandwich 20
  tire 83
  20th-century wooden covered-bridge 79
  wholesale packaged-bait dealer 53
  wooden sports dome 78
  year-round Christmas store 11

LONGEST
  freshwater stretch of sand dunes 31
  freshwater yachting course 50
  front porch 25

MOST
  replaced body joints 86

MOST-BEAUTIFUL
  masonic temple 78

MOST-COMPLETE
  mastodon trackway 92

MOST-FAMOUS
  sand dune 31

ONLY
  flyable collection of WWII "cats" 93
  Kirtland's Warbler breeding grounds 62
  vintage car meet 90

RECORD
  hot dog consumption 6

TALLEST
  and largest steel building imploded 86
  hotel 30
  indoor waterfall 43

THE AUTHOR

Gary W. Barfknecht, 54, was born and raised in Virginia, Minnesota, the "Queen City" of that state's Mesabi Iron Range. After receiving a bachelor of science degree from the University of Minnesota in 1967 and a master of science degree from the University of Washington in 1969, he came to Flint, Michigan, as a paint chemist with the E.I. DuPont & deNemours Company.

But after only a year on the job, Barfknecht and the chemical giant reached the mutual conclusion that he was not suited for corporate life, and Barfknecht set out on a freelance writing career. He sold the first magazine article he ever wrote, "Robots Join the Assembly Line" (*Science & Mechanics*, October 1971), and over the next three years, his articles were featured in *Reader's Digest, Science Digest, Lion, Sign, Lutheran Standard, Modern Maturity* and other magazines. He also was the ghost writer for the book, *A Father, A Son, and a Three Mile Run* (Zondervan, 1974) and authored and self-published a local guide book, *33 Hikes From Flint* (Friede Publications, 1975).

While freelancing, Barfknecht also managed a hockey pro shop at Flint's I.M.A. ice arena. In 1977 he suspended his writing efforts when he became director of almost all amateur hockey programming in the Genesee County area.

In 1981 he resigned as hockey commissioner to again become a fulltime author and publisher, and a year later he self-published what became a best-selling collection of Michigan trivia titled *Michillaneous*. Barfknecht followed with five other Michigan books: *Murder, Michigan* (1983), *Mich-Again's Day* (1984), *Michillaneous II* (1985), *Ultimate Michigan Adventures* (1989) and *Unexplained Michigan Mysteries* (1993).

As owner and Managing Editor of Friede Publica-

tions, Barfknecht has brought 17 books into print by other Michigan authors, including *A Traveler's Guide to 116 Michigan Lighthouses* and *A Guide to 199 Michigan Waterfalls* by the Penrose family, *Natural Michigan* and *Michigan State and National Parks: A Complete Guide* by Tom Powers, *Canoeing Michigan Rivers* by Jerry Dennis, and a six-volume Michigan fishing guide series by Tom Huggler.

After living in Davison for 27 years, Barfknecht and his wife, Ann, are relocating to Petoskey.

Daughter Heidi is an educator in the Washington D.C. area.

In Atlanta, daughter Amy and her husband, Dan, take good care of their son Anders (pictured above) between visits from grandma and grandpa. Anders is awaiting the arrival of his sister, due to enter the world shortly after this book goes to press.